GOPRO HERO 13 USER GUIDE

A BEGINNER'S MANUAL TO SETTING UP AND USING THE GOPRO HERO 13 CAMERA

REYNOLD HOPPS

LEGAL NOTICE

The information contained in this book is for information and educational purposes. No part of this book may be duplicated, transmitted, or distributed in any form or by any means, including photocopying, recording, and other mechanical or electronic methods, without the prior written permission of the publisher and the author, except in the case of brief quotations embodied in reviews and other non-commercial uses permitted by copyright law.

Copyright © 2024 Reynold Hopps

All Rights Reserved

TABLE OF CONTENT

- LEGAL NOTICE ... II
- TABLE OF CONTENT ... III
- INTRODUCTION ... VIII
- **CHAPTER ONE** ... 1
  - OVERVIEW OF THE GOPRO HERO 13 ... 1
    - About The GoPro Hero 13 ... 1
    - Comparing Video Quality and Stabilization with the Hero 12 ... 3
    - Audio and Microphone Support: Still Room for Improvement in the GoPro Hero 13 ... 4
    - New Accessories and Lens Mods: A Definite Win ... 5
    - Battery Life: A Welcome Boost in the GoPro Hero 13 (But With Trade-Offs) ... 6
    - Ideal uses for the GoPro Hero 13: Sports, travel, and professional videography ... 7
- **CHAPTER TWO** ... 11
  - GETTING STARTED WITH YOUR GOPRO HERO 13 ... 11
    - Unboxing the GoPro Hero 13 ... 11
      - Setting Up the Camera ... 12
    - Getting Familiar with the Accessories ... 12
      - Buttons, Ports, and Components ... 12
    - Understanding the GoPro Hero 13's interface ... 18
      - The Front Display Screen ... 18
      - The Rear Touchscreen ... 20
      - Voice Control ... 22
      - WIFI/Bluetooth ... 26
- **CHAPTER THREE** ... 29
  - THE GOPRO APP AND SHARING CONTENTS ... 29
    - Connecting your camera to the Quik the GoPro App ... 29
      - Getting to know the App Properly ... 30
      - How to control the Quik App ... 30
      - GoPro Subscription ... 31
    - How to Automatically Transfer Files Using Wi-Fi 6 ... 32
      - Ensure Wi-Fi 6 Compatibility ... 32
      - Connect your GoPro Hero 13 to Wi-Fi ... 32
      - Automatic File Transfer Setup ... 33
      - Process of Transferring Files ... 33
      - Editing within the GoPro App ... 33
      - Sharing Your Content ... 33
    - Color Correcting, Trimming, and Filtering Within-App ... 33
      - Color Correction ... 34
      - Trimming ... 34
      - Filtering ... 34
    - Sharing Your Content ... 35
      - How To Share Content Directly to Socials or Directly to the Cloud ... 35
      - Editing Your Content ... 35
      - Share Directly to Social Media ... 36

Upload Content Directly to the Cloud 36
Tips to Share and Back Up Efficiently 36

CHAPTER FOUR 37

UNDERSTANDING GOPRO HERO 13 CAMERA SETTINGS 37

Resolution and Frame Rate Options 37
Image Dimensions 38
Video Mode Aspect Ratio settings: 38
16:9 Aspect Ratio info: 38
4:3 Aspect Ratio info: 38
5.3K, 4K, 1080p: Which resolution to use and when 39
Practical Scenarios for Each Resolution 41
Frame rates explained: 24fps, 30fps, 60fps, 120fps 41
Practical Recommendations for Using Frame Rates 43

Low-light and HDR settings for enhanced performance in different environments 44
Low-Light Settings 44
HDR Settings for Improved Dynamic Range 45
Practical Tips for Low-Light and HDR Shooting 45

How to Set Up 4k/60fps Video Recording 46
Optimizing for Reduced Resolution 46

Storage and Battery Life Management 47

Post-Processing Considerations 47

QuikCapture mode: Instant recording with a single button press 47
How to Use GoPro QuickCapture 47

CHAPTER FIVE 49

LENS AND MODS 49

Introduction to Interchangeable Lenses and Mods 49
Getting Familiar with the New HB-Series Lenses 49
Snap and Go Magnetic Latch Mounting System 51
Why These Mods Matter 52

How to Shoot Using Ultra Wide, Macro, and Anamorphic Lens Mods 52
Ultra-Wide Lens Mod 52
Macro Lens Mod 53
Anamorphic Lens Mod 53

Attaching and Taking Off Mods 54
Attaching a Lens Mod 54
Removing a Lens Mod 54

Best Use of Each Lens Mod and Filter 55
Ultra-Wide Lens Mod 55
Macro Lens Mod 55
Anamorphic Lens Mod 55
ND Filter 4-Pack 56

CHAPTER SIX 57

ADVANCED FEATURES OF THE GOPRO HERO 13 57

An in-depth look at HyperSmooth 6.0 Stabilization and Horizon Lock 57
HyperSmooth 6.0: Unbreakable Stability 57
Horizon Lock: Maintaining Perfect Alignment 57

Video Stabilization ... 58
How to stabilize GoPro video after recording ... 59
Horizon Lock ... 60
How to Lock Orientation on the GoPro HERO 13 ... 60
Basic Orientation Lock ... 61
Enabling Landscape Lock on the HERO13 ... 62
When Automatic Rotation Detection can be Inconvenient ... 63
Things worth Knowing ... 64
SELF-TIMER ... 64

CHAPTER SEVEN ... 66

Exploring Photography with Hero 13 ... 66

Still Photography Options: Photo, Burst, and Live Burst Modes ... 66
Photographic Mode ... 66
Burst Slo-Mo ... 67
Performance: ... 67
How to Take Burst Slo-Mo Photos: ... 67
Live Burst Mode ... 67
How it Works: ... 68
Steps to Capture a Live Burst: ... 68
General Tips Applicable in All Modes: ... 68

Shooting Close-up with the Macro Lens Mod ... 68
Understanding the Macro Lens Mod ... 68
Attaching the Macro Lens Mod ... 69
Optimizing Camera Settings ... 69
Tips for Shooting Close-ups ... 69

Editing and Post-Processing ... 70
How to Shoot HDR and 10-bit Color Photos ... 70
Understanding HDR and 10-bit Color ... 70
How to Set Up Your GoPro Hero 13 to Shoot HDR and 10-bit Color Photos ... 70
Tips for Shooting HDR and 10-bit Color Photos ... 71

How to Shoot in Low Light and Night Modes ... 72
Low-Light Challenges Explained ... 72
Setting Up Low-Light Photography ... 72
Night Mode Shooting Tips ... 73

RAW mode for professional-level photo editing ... 73
Benefits of Shooting in RAW Mode ... 73
When to Use Raw Mode ... 74
How to Shoot in RAW with the GoPro Hero 13 ... 74
Considerations for Shooting in RAW ... 74

Live Streaming: Broadcasting directly to social media platforms from the camera ... 75
How to Set Up Live Streaming on the GoPro Hero 13 ... 75
Tips for a Better Live Streaming Experience ... 76
Using RTMP for Custom Streaming ... 76
Practical Scenarios for Live Streaming with the Hero 13 ... 77

CHAPTER EIGHT ... 77

Advanced Features and Settings ... 77

Checking Out GPS and Performance Data with Stickers ... 77
GPS and Performance Data Tracking ... 77

Working with Performance Stickers 78
How to Turn On GPS and Use Stickers 78
Performance Sticker Benefits 78
Sharing and Analyzing Your Data 79
How to Create Custom Presets Based on Environment 79
Understanding Key Settings 79
Creating Custom Presets 79
Optimization Presets for Specific Environments 80
Testing and Refining 81
Preset Backup and Sharing 81
Audio Tuning: How to Get the Right Balance Between Sound and Enhanced Voice Clarity 81
Balanced Sound Profile 81
Enhanced Voice Clarity Mode 81
Automatic Switching and Real-Time Adjustments 82
Multi-Microphone System 82
Practical Applications 82
Going Into ProTune: Exposure, White Balance, and ISO Manually 83
Exposure Control 83
White Balance 83
ISO Settings 83
Using ProTune for Professional Results 84

CHAPTER NINE 85

ADVANCED CINEMATOGRAPHY TECHNIQUES 85

Filmmaking with the Hero 13: From Action Sequences to Documentaries 85
Using High-Resolution Capabilities 85
Professional Level Color Grading with HLG HDR 85
Creative Use of Time-Lapse and Slo-Mo Mode 86
Tapping into Audio Personalisation for Documentaries 86
Practical Mounting Solutions 86
Cinematic Techniques: Using the Anamorphic Lens Mod on Shooting of Movie-Style Footage 87
Understanding the Anamorphic Lens Mod 87
Techniques of Shooting with Anamorphic Lens 87
Maximize Features on GoPro Hero 13 87
Post-Production Tips 88
Practical Applications 88
How to Use Slow-Motion Creatively in Storytelling 88
    Highlighting Significant Events 88
    Create Suspense and Tension 89
    Improving Emotional Impact 89
    Details with Macro Shots 89
    Shooting Epic Action Shots 89
    Enhancing the Cinematic Feel with Anamorphic Lenses 90
    Telling a Story Through Visual Contrast 90
    Using Sound Design in Slow-Motion 90
Key Takeaways 90
Working with Other Gear: Drones, Gimbals, and External Microphones 90
Drones: Aerial Cinematography 90
Gimbals: Stabilized Ground Footage 91
External Microphones: Improved Audio Quality 91

CHAPTER TEN — 93

Mounting Your GoPro Hero 13 — 93

Overview of GoPro mounts and accessories — 93
- Magnetic Latch Mounting System — 93
- Built-In Mounting Fingers — 93
- 1/4-20 Mounting Threads — 94
- Underwater and adventure use: Preparing your GoPro for extreme conditions — 94
- Using GoPro Mods (Media Mod, Light Mod, Display Mod) to expand functionality — 96
  - Media Mod — 96
  - Light Mod — 97
  - Display Mod — 98
- Tips for Using GoPro Mods Together — 98
- Best Mounts for Different Activities: Cycling, Surfing, Hiking, etc. — 98
  - Cycling — 98
  - Surfing — 99
  - Hiking — 99
  - Snowboarding and skiing — 99
  - Diving — 100
- Power and Mounting Accessories: Volta grip, Ball Joint Mount — 100
  - Volta Power Grip — 100
  - Ball Joint Mount — 101
- Other Mount Accessories — 101
- DIY Mounting Hacks and Ideas to Capture Unique Perspectives — 102
  - Snap and Go Magnetic Latch Mounting System — 102
  - DIY Hack: Magnetic Mount on Metal Surfaces — 102
  - Ball Joint Mounts — 102
  - DIY Hack: Custom Swivel Mount — 102
  - Built-in Mounting Fingers and 1/4-20 Mounting Threads — 102
  - DIY Hack: Helmet Mounting — 102
  - HB-Series Lens Mods — 102
  - DIY Hack: Handheld Rig with Lens Mods — 103
  - Suction Cup and Clamp Mounts — 103
  - DIY Hack: Custom Suction Mount — 103
  - DIY Hack: Custom Shoulder Mount — 104
  - Additional Tips — 104

CONCLUSION — 105
INDEX — 106

INTRODUCTION

The 2024 introduction of the GoPro Hero 13 is a testament to the brand's commitment to producing action cameras that are both durable and high-performing. This model is renowned for its ability to capture breathtaking footage in the most difficult environments. It has been improved in a variety of ways, rendering it more user-friendly and versatile than its predecessors.

Whether you are a fan of extreme sports, vlogging, or simply enjoy capturing the ordinary moments of life, the Hero 13 has the features to meet your needs. It is designed to withstand any adventure you can present it with, thanks to the inclusion of sophisticated lens mods, enhanced video capabilities, and an extended battery life.

This guide will provide you with comprehensive information on how to optimize your Hero 13. Let us commence with the fundamentals: the camera's unboxing and configuration. You will become acquainted with the primary controls, settings, and menu options, which are essential for ensuring that you are prepared to record in any circumstance.

The interface of the Hero 13 is uncomplicated; however, it offers a plethora of customization options for users who desire greater control over their footage. To ensure that you are at ease with the device before pressing the record button, we will provide a detailed explanation of the functions of each setting and how to navigate the camera's touchscreen.

Lastly, the guide will provide instructions on how to optimize GoPro's mobile app and editing software for post-production. We will provide a detailed guide on how to transfer footage, alter videos, and add the final flourishes. Practical editing guidelines are provided to improve your content, regardless of whether you are striving to create a professional-grade video or a humorous film for social media.

The completion of this guide will provide you with a comprehensive comprehension of the effective and creative use of the Hero 13, allowing you to capture high-quality footage in any environment. Regardless of whether you are a novice or an experienced GoPro user, this guide contains valuable information to assist you in optimizing your new action camera.

CHAPTER ONE
OVERVIEW OF THE GOPRO HERO 13

About The GoPro Hero 13

The GoPro Hero 13 Black, which was introduced in September 2024, is the most recent addition to GoPro's action camera lineup. It retains a design that is comparable to the Hero 12 Black, but it incorporates several significant improvements:

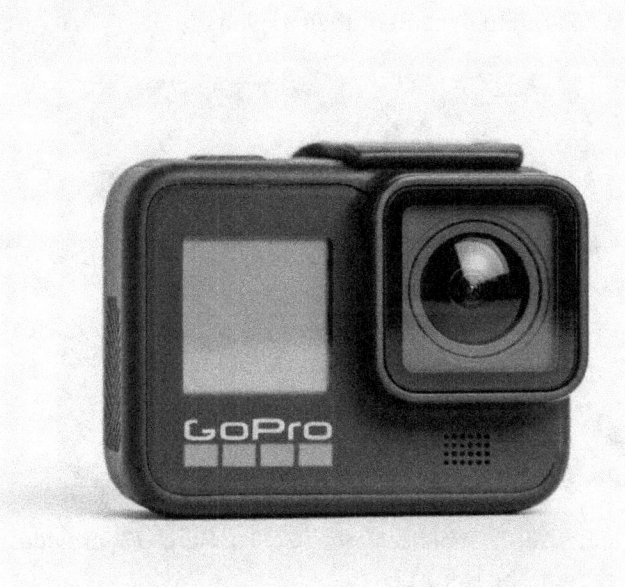

1. **Video and Camera Performance:** The Hero 13 is equipped with a 27-megapixel sensor that is capable of recording 5.3K video at a maximum frame rate of 120fps and slow-motion at 720p at a rate of 400fps. Although the sensor has not been altered from the previous model, it is suitable for capturing fast-paced action due to its new Burst Slo-Mo mode and improved stabilization.
2. **New Lens Mod System:** It introduces the HB-Series lens modifications, which facilitate the effortless exchange of various lens varieties. Some of the options available are an ultra-wide, macro, and ND filter lens. The camera automatically detects the lens attached to it and adjusts the settings accordingly, thereby increasing the camera's adaptability to a variety of shooting scenarios.
3. **Enhanced Thermal Management and Battery Life:** The new 1,900mAh Enduro battery provides approximately 13.5% more battery life and substantial enhancements in heat management, enabling extended recording periods at higher resolutions.

4. **Additional Features:** GPS functionality is reinstated to mark location data, and a new audio tuning feature has been implemented to enhance voice capture. The mounting system is also upgraded to include a new magnetic clasp that facilitates faster attachment and release.

I can confidently assert that the GoPro Hero 13 is a solid upgrade with a few thrilling enhancements, having tested it for a few weeks. Nevertheless, there are certain areas in which GoPro could have improved, and I will elaborate on them in the subsequent sections of this article.

To provide context, I have been utilizing **GoPro`s** since 2007, and this most recent model serves as further evidence that they are indispensable tools for individuals who prefer to film independently, as well as content creators and those who wish to document their exploits.

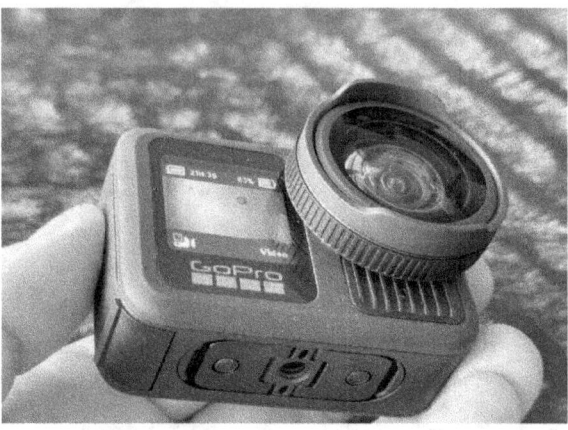

In terms of functionality and user-friendliness, the GoPro Hero 13 provides numerous significant enhancements over its antecedent, the Hero 12.

The introduction of electronic communication between the camera and the lens modifications is one of the most remarkable developments. This feature eliminates the necessity of manually adjusting the camera settings when exchanging lenses, which was a minor inconvenience in the past. Therefore, this is a significant improvement on a camera of this nature if you frequently alter your shooting technique, such as transitioning from wide-angle action photos to close-up macro work.

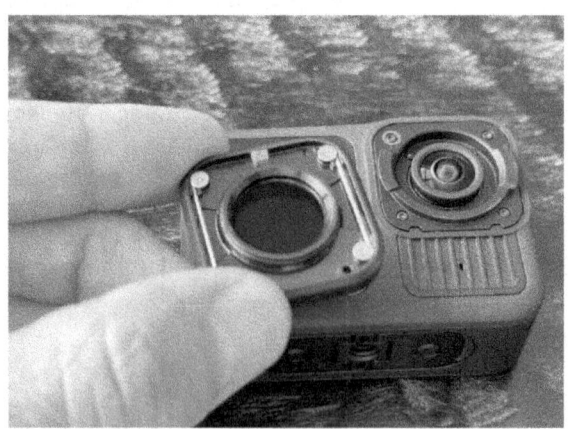

Additionally, the Hero 13 incorporates an enhanced magnetic quick-release plate that enables users to rapidly switch between attachments. This is particularly beneficial for activities that require a high level of speed, such as off-roading or mountain bicycling. This magnetic fast release has a significantly more secure feel than others I have tested in the past, and I commend GoPro for this.

The thermal efficacy is another noteworthy enhancement. The endurance of the GoPro Hero 13 is approximately 13.5% longer than that of the Hero 12, as it is equipped with a 1900mAh Enduro battery and a new radiator. An extended period between charges? Scotty, please transport me to the heavens.

The battery is more resilient to both hot and chilly environments, while the enhanced heat dissipation helps prevent overheating if you typically shoot in extreme conditions, whether that's hot desert days or frigid winter evenings. The disadvantage of this new battery is that it is not backward-compatible with previous models. This can be a source of frustration for those who have already purchased multiple GoPro batteries. I have a significant number of batteries that are incompatible with the Hero 13, as GoPro has not replaced them since the release of the Hero 9.

Comparing Video Quality and Stabilization with the Hero 12

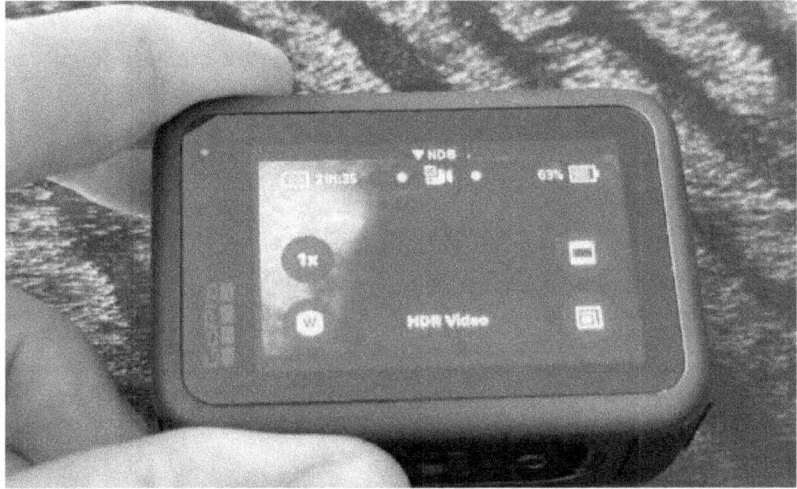

Perhaps one of the most significant drawbacks of the GoPro Hero 13 is that it retains the same sensor as the Hero 12. This is for video quality. The sensor is beginning to exhibit its age, particularly in low-light situations, even though the 8:7 aspect ratio remains distinctive and beneficial for capturing immersive footage.

The Hero 13 outperforms other action cameras on the market by capturing clear, crisp footage that is comparable to those of the best in well-lit environments. Nevertheless, the limitations of this aging sensor become more apparent as illumination conditions deteriorate. The colors begin to decline in vibrancy, and the footage begins to appear pixelated.

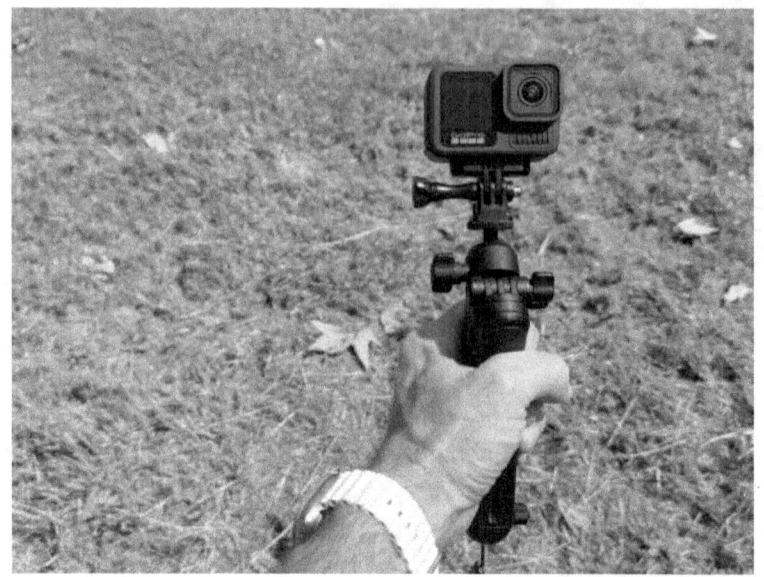

The HyperSmooth 6.0 technology in the GoPro Hero 13 is still one of the most effective stabilization technologies available on any action camera. It is an incremental enhancement to the Hero 12's HyperSmooth 5.0, which is already exceptional, and provides smoother footage even in challenging conditions.

Most of the footage I record is while driving my Jeep Gladiator down off-road trails with the camera mounted on the bonnet or front fender. I must commend GoPro for its exceptional image stabilization. Nevertheless, the stabilization's efficacy is somewhat contingent upon the illumination conditions, as is the case with the camera's low-light performance. In low light, it appears to be diminished. GoPro's competitors, such as the DJI Osmo Action, are beginning to catch up in this area.

Audio and Microphone Support: Still Room for Improvement in the GoPro Hero 13

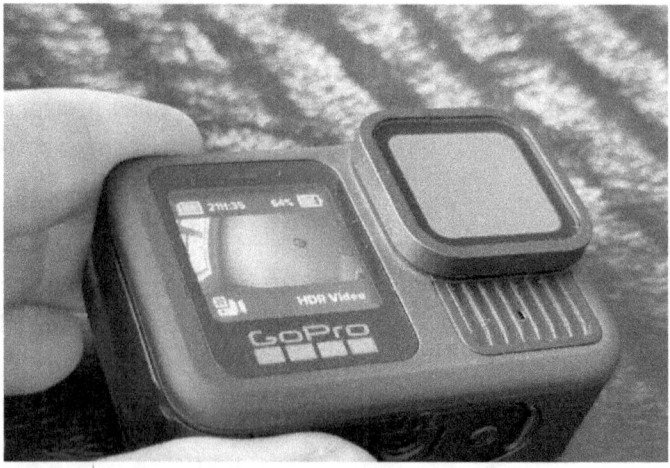

The absence of wireless microphone support in the Hero 13 is one of the most significant lost opportunities in my opinion. Although the internal audio quality is satisfactory, it is inadequate when compared to the quality of professional-grade sound that can be obtained through the use of external equipment.

GoPro has made some progress by incorporating a Voice Audio mode that prioritizes voice-over ambient sound; however, this is insufficient. Bluetooth support for renowned wireless microphones, such as the Rode Wireless Pro, would be greatly appreciated by numerous creators, myself included. This would have been an exceptional feature for vloggers and solitary shooters.

Full disclosure: the GoPro Hero 13 can still be used with an external microphone, such as the Rode Wireless Pro. Nevertheless, it is necessary to utilize a device such as their Media Mod Kit and connect the Rode Wireless Pro to the 3.5mm interface. Is this functional? Yes. Is it convenient? No. Regrettably, the inclusion of Bluetooth support for wireless microphones would necessitate hardware modifications rather than merely a software update. Consequently, it is improbable that GoPro will be able to resolve this issue through a firmware update. Alternatively, I anticipate that GoPro will either incorporate this feature into future models or create its wireless microphone system.

New Accessories and Lens Mods: A Definite Win

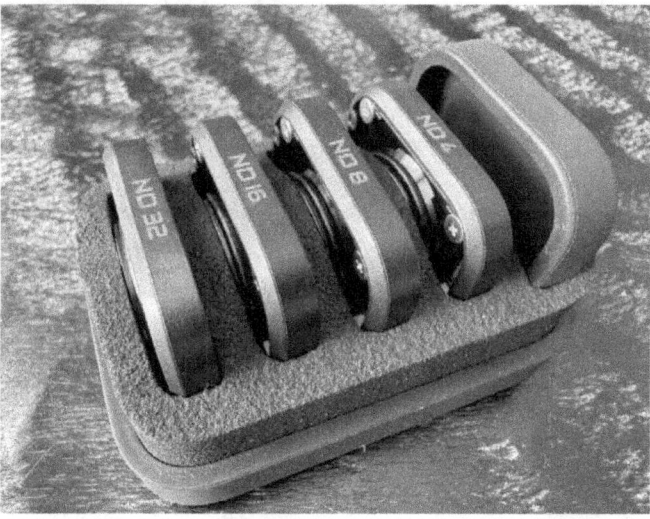

The new lens modifications are one area in which GoPro has excelled. Previously, interchangeable lenses were unable to communicate with the camera; however, the GoPro Hero 13 alleviates this issue. The camera can now automatically adjust settings for specific lens modifications, such as ultra-wide, macro, and ND filters, which adds a level of versatility that older models simply did not possess.

For example, the ultra-wide variant is an excellent choice for capturing expansive landscapes or POV action photos. It is perfect for activities such as hiking, cycling, or snorkeling, as its 177-degree field of view captures nearly everything in front of the camera. The ultra-wide variant of the Hero 13 is particularly remarkable due to its horizon leveling feature, which ensures that the horizon remains upright even when the camera rotates.

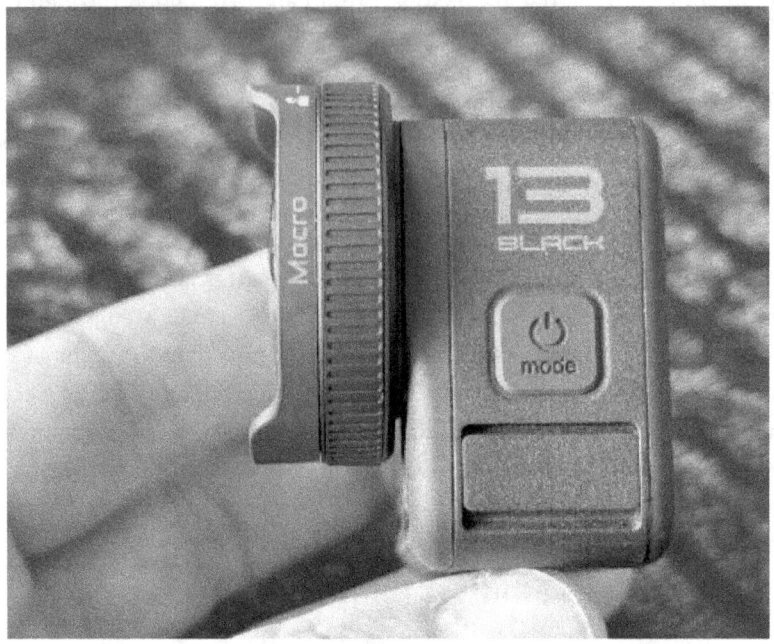

Another thrilling addition to the GoPro Hero 13 is the macro lens retrofit. These cameras have historically been wide-angle, with a fixed focus that has impeded the ability to capture close-up images. The macro mod enables a focus as close as 4.33 inches, which expands the scope of creative opportunities.

This represents an enormous advantage for nature photographers or individuals who wish to capture the intricate details of tiny objects. The camera also includes a new ND filter set that automatically adjusts settings to achieve the desired motion blur effect, thereby simplifying the process of capturing cinematic footage.

Battery Life: A Welcome Boost in the GoPro Hero 13 (But With Trade-Offs)

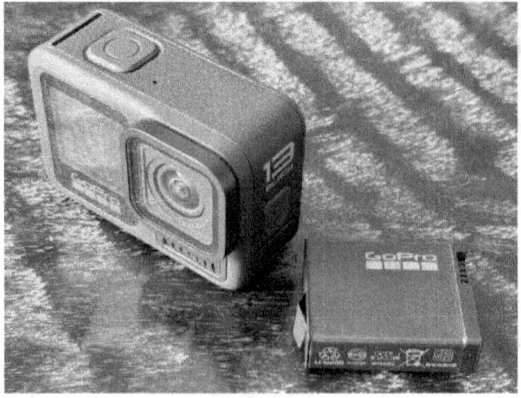

Compared to the Hero 12's battery performance, the new 1900mAh Enduro battery provides a clear improvement. I discovered that I could photograph continuously for an extended period without experiencing concerns about the camera overheating or the battery expiring prematurely. This is a substantial improvement for individuals who utilize the GoPro for extended periods, whether on a multi-day adventure or an all-day session. The battery is also expected to operate more efficiently in colder temperatures, a fact that I will verify as winter approaches. I am eager to observe the GoPro Hero 13 battery's performance in low-temperature conditions, as this was a weakness in previous GoPro models.

Nevertheless, as previously stated, the Enduro battery is incompatible with previous GoPro models. Consequently, if you are upgrading from an older camera, such as the Hero 10 or Hero 12, you will be required to purchase entirely new batteries. This can be a deterrent for certain users, as it increases the cost.

Ideal uses for the GoPro Hero 13: Sports, travel, and professional videography

The GoPro Hero 13 is designed to perform exceptionally in a diverse array of environments, owing to its advanced features, flexible mounting options, and rugged construction. It is the best instrument for professional videography, travel, and sports due to its capacity to capture high-quality footage in challenging conditions. The following are the specific areas in which the Hero 13 excels:

1. **Sports**

Athletes and action sports devotees who desire to record dynamic footage from their perspective are particularly fond of the GoPro Hero 13. It is appropriate for a diverse array of sports due to its durable construction and compact size:

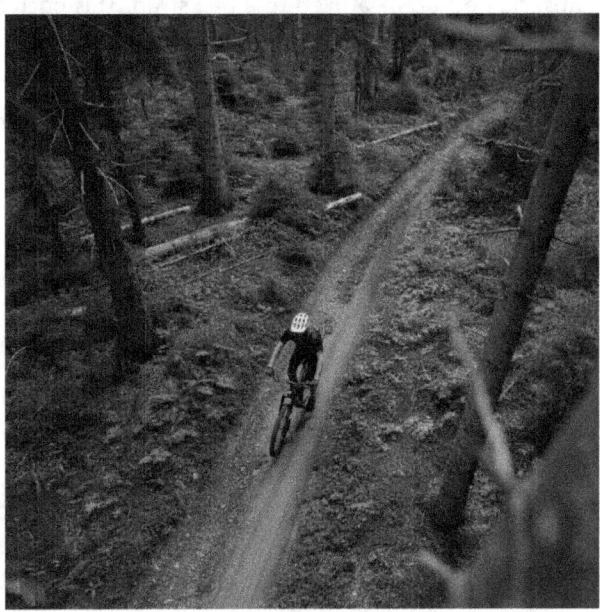

- **Extreme Sports:** The Hero 13's image stabilization technology (HyperSmooth 6.0) ensures that footage remains smooth and stable, even in fast-paced action or on rugged terrains, for activities such as mountain biking, skateboarding, surfing, and snowboarding. It is ideal for watersports due to its watertight design, which enables users to capture immersive underwater videos without the need for an external casing, up to 33 feet (10 meters).
- **Slow Motion and Burst-Shooting:** The camera's capacity to capture slow-motion footage at 120fps in 5.3K resolution and up to 400fps at 720p is excellent for the analysis of rapid movements. This is advantageous for athletes who wish to evaluate their form or technique, as well as for the creation of dramatic slow-motion films that emphasize critical moments in a sport, such as a leap, trick, or dive.
- **Mounting Flexibility:** The Hero 13 can be securely affixed to nearly any piece of equipment with the help of options such as helmet mounts, torso harnesses, and handlebar mounts. This adaptability enables the capture of dynamic perspectives and inventive shot angles that are not feasible with a conventional camera.
- **Data Overlays and GPS:** The reintroduction of GPS functionality allows athletes to overlay real-time data, including pace, altitude, and distance, onto their recordings. This function is advantageous for sports such as skiing, cycling, and motorsports, as it provides an additional layer of information to the footage through performance metrics.

2. **Travel**

The Hero 13 offers a portable and lightweight solution for travelers to capture memories while on the go. It is a dependable travel companion due to its sophisticated features and durable design:

- **Portability and Compactness:** The camera's diminutive size enables it to be effortlessly transported in a knapsack, pocket, or affixed to a bag strap. This portability is ideal for travelers who desire to document their excursions in high quality while also packing light.
- **Low-Light Performance:** Although the Hero 13 was not specifically designed for nocturnal photography, its enhanced software-based features enable it to capture high-quality footage in low-light conditions. It is beneficial for indoor environments, dimly-lit streets, or sunset scenes.
- **Wide Field of View:** The Hero 13's ultra-wide lens adaptation enables travelers to capture expansive landscapes and cityscapes, resulting in immersive footage that can cover a greater area than typical cameras. This lens is particularly advantageous for capturing picturesque landscapes or bustling markets.
- **TimeWarp and Time-Lapse:** The camera's integrated TimeWarp and time-lapse modes allow users to produce breathtaking travel sequences that condense lengthy events into brief, shareable segments. This is an excellent tool for documenting the movement of individuals in a crowded area, as well as road excursions and treks.
- **Mounting Ease:** The Hero 13 can be quickly attached and detached from a variety of locations, such as a vehicle dashboard, selfie stick, or shoulder strap, thanks to quick-mount options like the magnetic latch. This enables travelers to quickly transition between different shooting setups.

3. **Professional Videography**

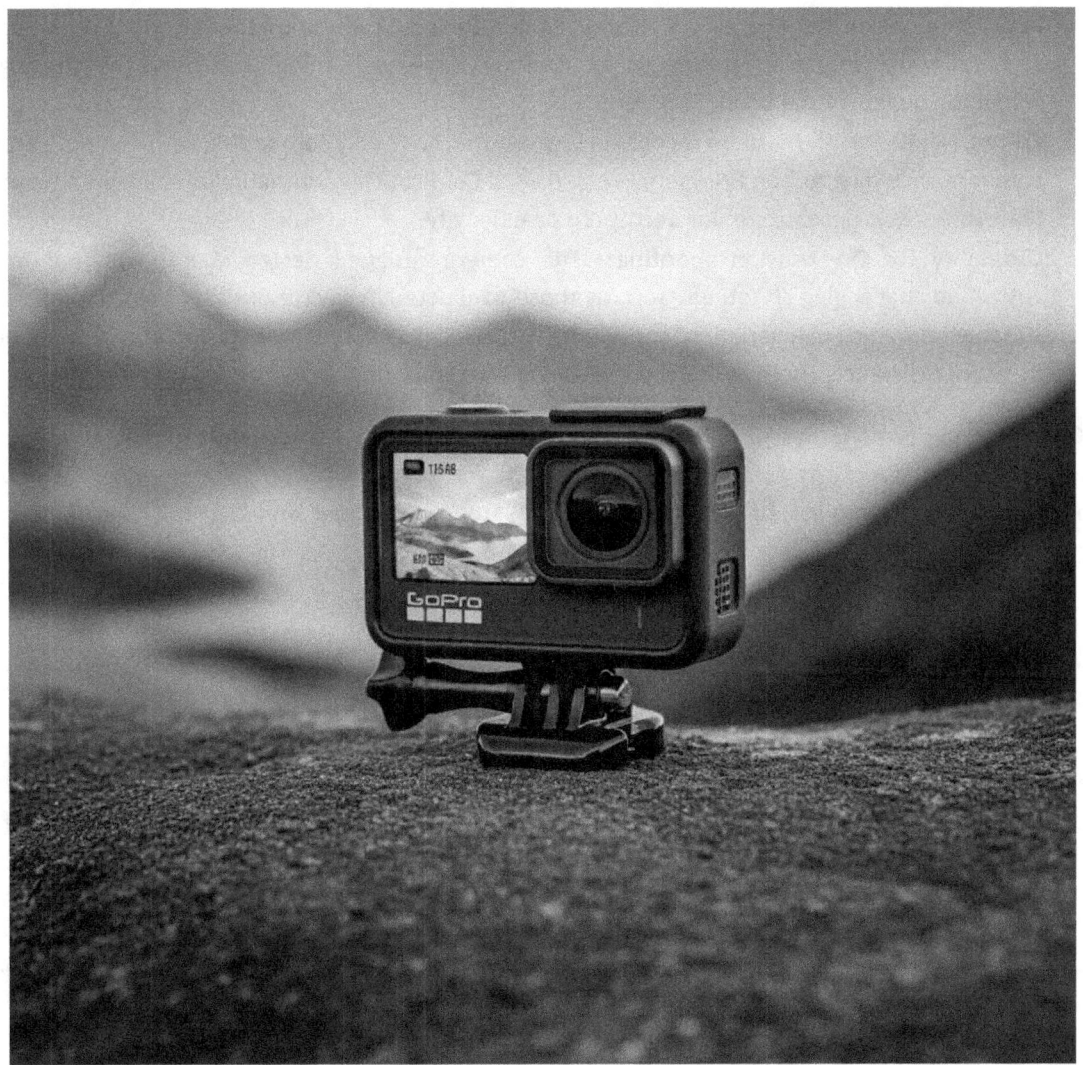

The Hero 13 is primarily recognized as an action camera, but it also includes features that are beneficial to professional videographers:

- **High-Resolution Video and Image Quality:** The Hero 13 is capable of producing professional-quality recordings, as it supports 5.3K video at 60fps and 27-megapixel images. Its capacity to capture footage at high frame rates offers the necessary adaptability for post-production, enabling editors to produce slow-motion effects that are more fluid.
- **Interchangeable Lens Mods:** The new HB-Series lenses, which include macro and ND filters, provide professionals with greater control over the appearance of their footage. For example, the macro lens allows for close-up photos of small objects with manual focusing capabilities, while the ND filters assist in regulating exposure in bright illumination. Filmmakers will be able to achieve a cinematic aspect ratio with lens flares for a classic movie appearance with the forthcoming anamorphic lens retrofit.

- **Audio Improvements:** The Hero 13 boasts enhanced audio calibration that prioritizes voices over ambient noise. This is advantageous for documentary-style filming, interviews, or vlogging, in which the quality of the sound is essential.
- **Editing Flexibility:** The camera records in formats that are easily compatible with common editing software, including Adobe Premiere Pro and Final Cut Pro. This compatibility is advantageous for filmmakers who necessitate uninterrupted productivity.
- **Durability for On-Location shootings:** The camera's rugged design guarantees that it can withstand challenging shootings, such as those conducted in severe outdoor environments. It is suitable for filming in a variety of conditions, including tropical rainforests and arid dunes, due to its shock resistance, thermal management, and waterproofing.

The GoPro Hero 13 is more than just an action camera, as it combines professional capabilities with user-friendly features. It functions as a versatile instrument for individuals who wish to generate visually appealing content, regardless of whether it pertains to professional endeavors, travel, or sports.

CHAPTER TWO
Getting Started with Your GoPro Hero 13

Unboxing the GoPro Hero 13

The act of unboxing a GoPro Hero 13 is an exhilarating experience that provides an introduction to the most recent features and accessories of this adaptable action camera. The contents of the box and the process for initiating the process are as follows:

What is Included?

The following items will be present when the parcel is opened:

1. **GoPro Hero 13 Camera:** The primary feature of the GoPro Hero 13 Camera is its rugged, well-known design. It is suitable for a variety of recording environments due to its 27-megapixel sensor and the capacity to capture 5.3K video.
2. **Enduro Battery (1,900mAh):** The Hero 13 is equipped with a novel Enduro battery that provides a longer battery life than previously available variants. It is intended to accommodate prolonged recording sessions in difficult environments, such as extreme temperatures.
3. **Protective Lens Cover:** This serves to protect the camera's lens from grime and blemishes when it is not in use. The cover is readily removable to facilitate the attachment of various lens modifications.
4. **Accessories for Mounting:**
   - **Quick Release Mounting Buckle:** This buckle enables the camera to be securely attached to a variety of mounts, including helmet mounts, tripods, and torso harnesses.
   - **Curved Adhesive Mount:** This mount enables the camera to be affixed to curved surfaces, such as helmets, thereby ensuring stability for action photos.
   - **Magnetic Latch (optional):** In certain packages, a magnetic latch mount can be included for rapid attachment and release. This feature is especially useful for fast mounting during action scenes.
5. **USB-C Charging Cable:** This cable is utilized to transfer data to a computer and recharge the camera's battery.
6. **Quick Start Guide and Safety Instructions:** The box also contains rudimentary documentation to assist in the setup of the camera and the comprehension of critical safety protocols. Additionally, it includes a Quick Start Guide and Safety Instructions. The guide delineates the process of mounting the camera, connecting the battery, and initiating fundamental settings.

Setting Up the Camera

1. **Insert the Battery**: Begin by accessing the battery compartment, which is typically situated at the bottom or side of the camera. Ensure that the Enduro battery is inserted securely and that the compartment is closed tightly to preserve the impermeable closure.
2. **Battery Charging:** Utilize the USB-C cable that is supplied to recharge the battery. It is advisable to completely charge the battery before using the camera for the first time.
3. **Attach the Protective Lens or Lens Mode:** Simply ensure that the standard protective lens is securely secured if you are using it. Attach the protective lens or lens mod. Attach one of the new lens modifications, such as the macro or ND filters, by twisting it into position if you intend to use it. The Hero 13 will automatically detect the lens and adjust the camera settings accordingly.
4. **MicroSD Card Installation:** Ensure that a microSD card that is compatible with the device is inserted into the port designated for the storage of videos and photos. It is advisable to use a high-speed card when capturing high-resolution footage.
5. **Power On the Camera:** Turn on the camera by tapping the power/mode icon. The initial configuration can be completed by following the on-screen instructions, which include selecting your language, setting the date and time, and connecting to the GoPro app, once it has been turned on.

Getting Familiar with the Accessories

The camera can be utilized in a variety of scenarios with the assistance of the mounting accessories that are included. For example, the quick-release fastener is versatile and can be affixed to a variety of accessories, such as chest mounts or selfie sticks, to provide distinctive perspectives. Additionally, the curved adhesive mount is well-suited for helmets. During on-the-go shooting, utilize the magnetic fastener if it is included in your package for effortless and rapid attachment.

Upon completion of the unwrapping and setup process, you are prepared to begin capturing your adventures and examining the features of the Hero 13.

Buttons, Ports, and Components

This section explains the GoPro Hero 13's buttons, interfaces, and components.

1. **The Shutter Button**: This device is activated to initiate and conclude recording, as well as to capture images.

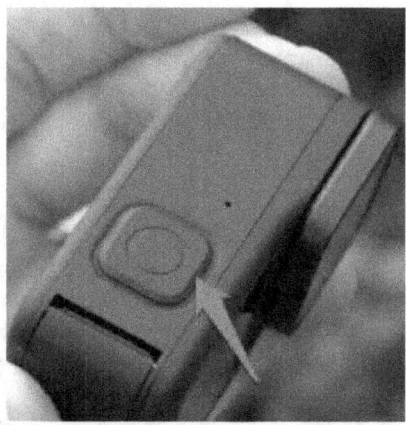

2. **The Camera Status Lights:** The status LEDs of the camera are red and serve as indicators. They appear during the recording or shooting process. There are two Camera Status Lights: one is located at the front and the other at the rear. The Preferences Menu allows you to disable them individually or collectively.

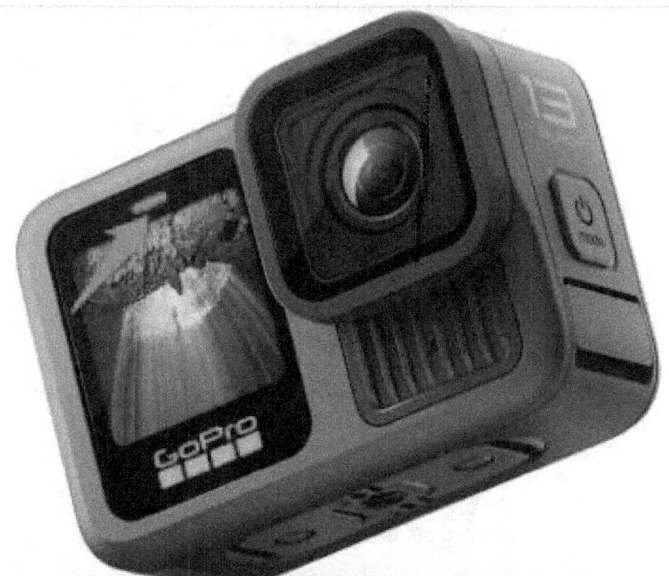

3. **Front Display Screen:** This screen displays your compositions. There is also a preview of the camera's settings.

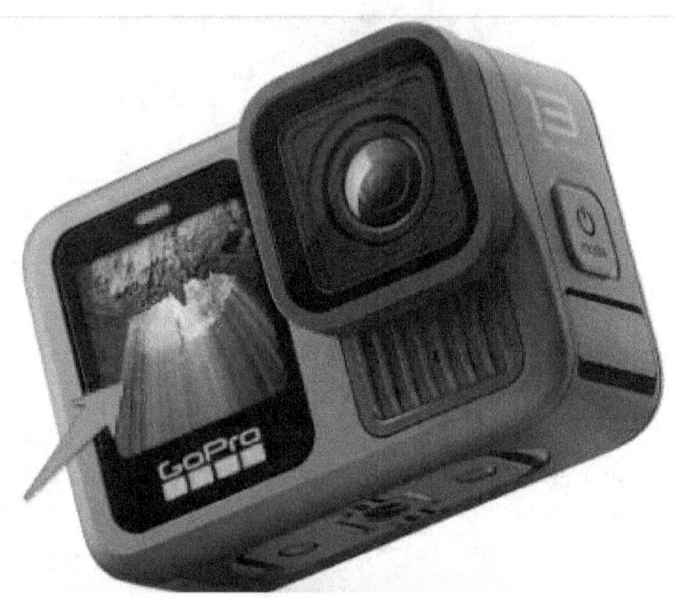

4. **Microphones:** These microphones are waterproof and are capable of recording stereo sound.

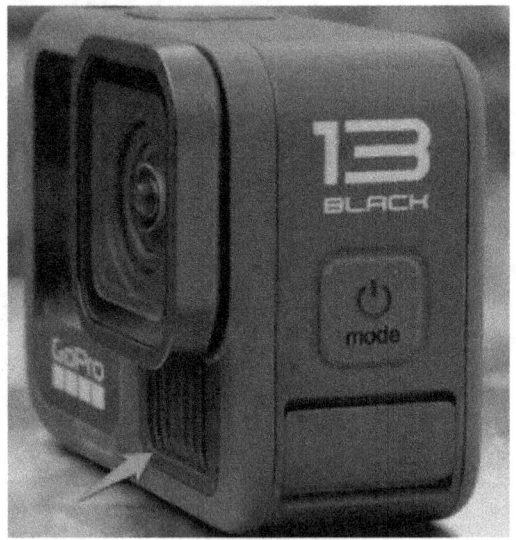

5. **The Microphone Drain:** This is a section of Hero 13 that enables water to escape from the microphone after immersing it in water or diving.

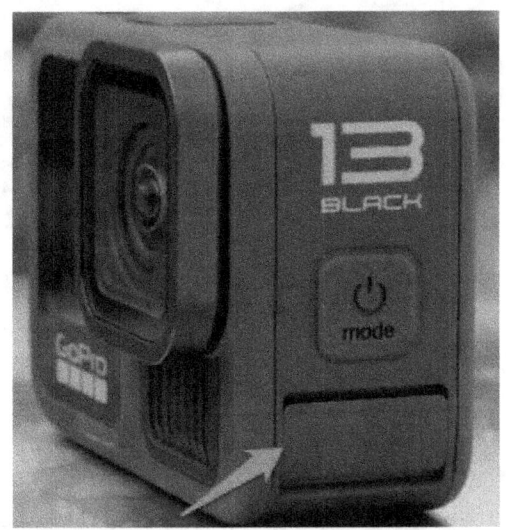

6. **The Power/Mode Button:** Press the Power button to activate the camera. Additionally, this device functions as the Mode device. The icon for scrolling through various modes is this one. This icon is also utilized to exit or exit the Settings or Media Screens, allowing for a swift return to shooting modes. Press and hold this button for four seconds to toggle the camera off.

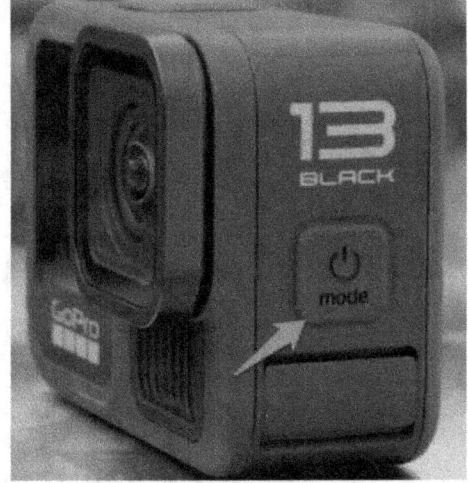

7. **Hydrophobic Lens Cover/Water Repellent Lens:** This lens cover is composed of glass and serves to safeguard the lens of your camera by preventing scratches and grime accumulation. If the lens cover is damaged, it can be replaced. To add filters or utilize the Max Lens Mod, it is possible to detach it by gently drawing it up and rotating it in a counterclockwise direction.

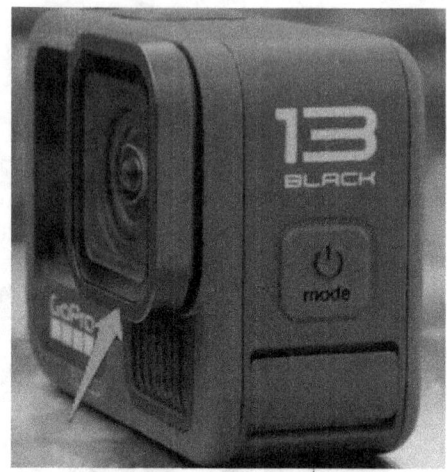

8. **The Rear Touch Screen:** The rear touch screen is a built-in LCD screen that serves a variety of functions, including serving as a selector and for setting adjustments, as a viewfinder for composing pictures, and for previewing previously recorded photos and videos.

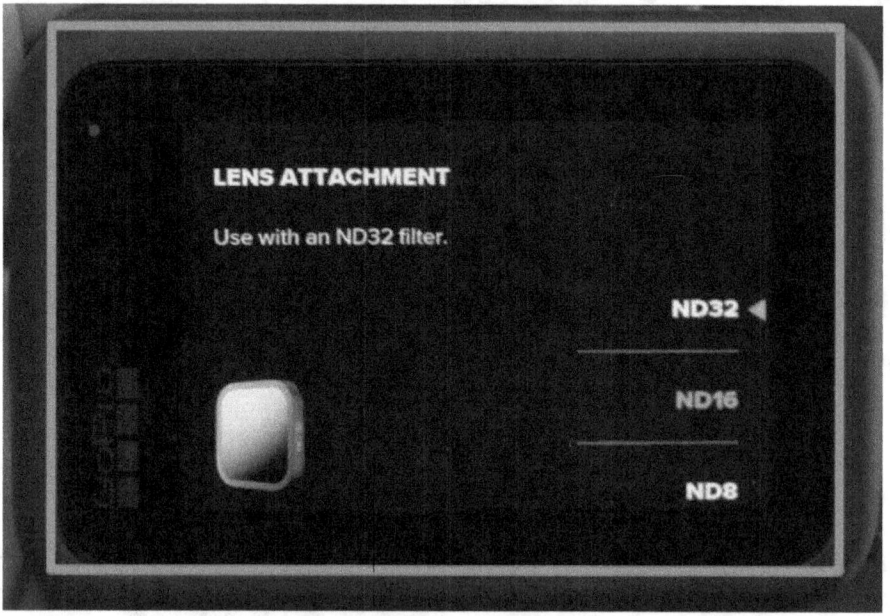

9. **The Speaker:** The speaker is responsible for playing the sound of a video when it is being previewed.

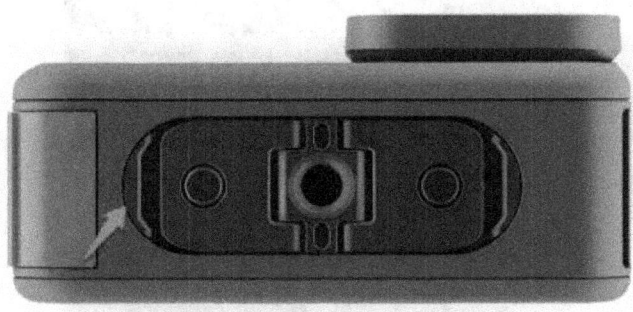

10. **The Mounting Fingers:** This component is utilized to secure your camera to mounts and can also be bent to allow the camera to be used unmounted.

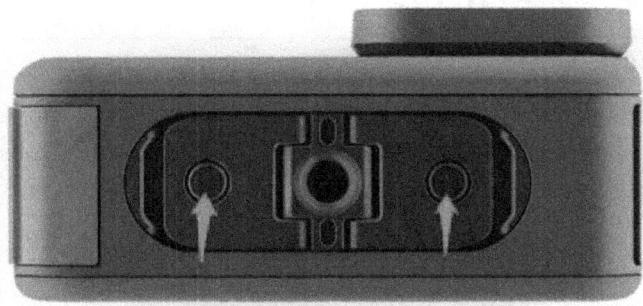

11. **The Battery Compartment, Memory Slot, and USB Port:** To install or remove the rechargeable battery, open the battery compartment door. The memory card is also stored in this compartment. The USB port is situated beneath this compartment. The USB port is utilized to attach the camera to the computer and to charge the camera. The compartment cover is detachable. The rubber gasket on the compartment door prevents water droplets from entering the camera; therefore, it is crucial to ensure that it is securely closed.

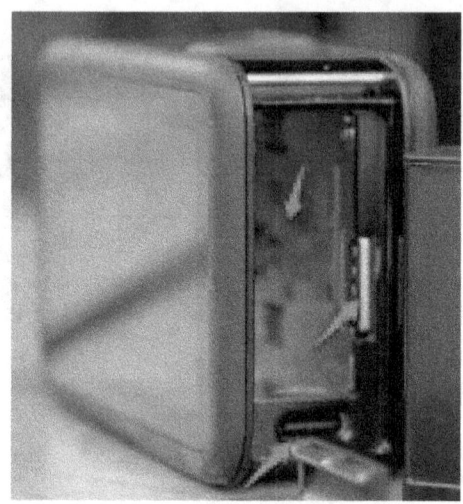

Understanding the GoPro Hero 13's interface

The Front Display Screen

The Front Display Screen provides a wealth of essential information regarding the status, settings, and modes of your camera. The Front Display Screen also provides the ability to observe a live view of your composition through the camera lens. The Front Screen is extremely beneficial for capturing shots or for selfies.

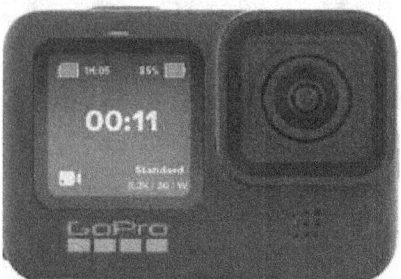

The Display Options for the Front Screen

The Front Display Icon on the Dashboard allows for the selection of one of four distinct display options for the front screen. Pulling down the dashboard from the top of the Rear Touch Screen will modify the display configuration for the Front Screen. The **Front Display Icon** is located in the bottom row. Simply tap it.

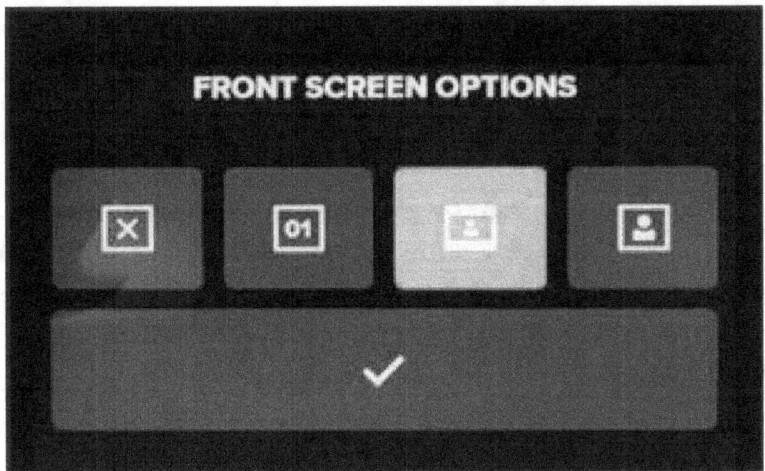

There are four options available.

1. **Off:** This option disables the front screen. This conserves the battery life of the camera when the front screen is not required.
2. **Status:** This option only displays the settings icons, not a live view through the camera lens.
3. **Actual Screen:** This option provides a comprehensive view of the entire video frame of your current recording, which is particularly useful for photographing.
4. **Full Screen:** This option provides a cropped view of the center of the camera frame. This alternative is highly advantageous due to its ability to optimize centered projectiles.

A concise summary of the functions of the icons on your camera's settings, modes, and status is provided below:

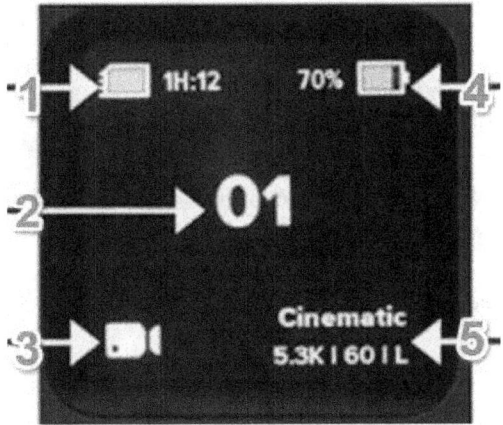

1. **Memory Card Capacity:** The memory card icon indicates the number of minutes that can be recorded on the memory card at the present video resolution. The time will also change when the parameters are altered, as a new resolution necessitates a different memory capacity. The icon will indicate the number of photos remaining when you are in the Photo Modes.

2. **The Counter:** In the Video Mode, it will display the quantity of videos that have been recorded. The duration of the video being recorded will be indicated by the time counter. Subsequently, the counter will indicate the total number of photographs that you have captured in Photo Mode.
3. **The Mode Icon:** This icon indicates the current recording mode, which is either Video, Photo, or Time Lapse.
4. **The Battery Life Indicator Icon:** This icon displays the current battery life percentage.
5. **The Settings Icon:** This icon displays the name of the Preset, the recording settings for a specific Preset, including the video resolution (5.3k, 4k, 1080, etc.), the video frame rate (30, 60, 120, etc.) or Interval (Burst and Time Lapse Modes), and the Digital Lens (Horizontal Lock, Hyper View, Super View, Wide, Linear).

The Rear Touchscreen

The Rear Touch Screen of the Hero 13 is an exceptional feature of the camera that was not present in the previous iterations of GoPro cameras. The Rear Touch Screen enables the preview of your photographs and also allows you to observe the impact of the settings on your videos and images in Live View. To safeguard the Touch Screen from scratches caused by accidents or impacts with abrasive objects, a screen protector is available.

Tip: The touch screen will not function correctly when your hands are damp, regardless of whether you are surfing, wearing snow or biking mittens. In those situations, it is recommended that you utilize the controls to modify the settings, as illustrated in the preceding section. Additionally, the touch screen's ability to modify settings can still be influenced by certain mounting positions.

Although you have acquired the ability to navigate the Touch Screen by altering settings, there are additional methods to optimize its functionality. The information that follows will provide additional light on the matter.

The Rear Touch Screen serves three primary functions:

- It serves as a selector and allows for the modification of parameters.
- It serves as a viewfinder.
- To view the photos and videos that were captured
- As a selector and for changing settings

As previously mentioned, the Rear Touch Screen is capable of selecting all modes and modifying settings.

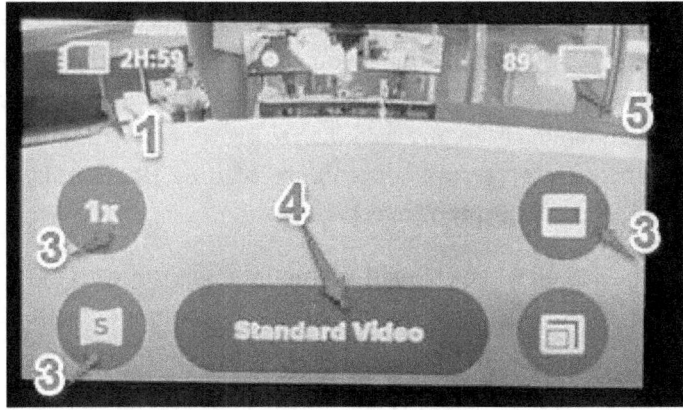

The following information will be displayed on the rear touch screen:

1. **The Camera Mode:** This icon indicates the current recording mode.
2. The Memory Card's capacity is equivalent to that of the **Front Screen Display**.
3. **Customizable On-Screen Shortcuts**: In a specific Preset, customizable on-screen shortcuts are always available. The icons displayed herein vary depending on the Preset that has been chosen. These shortcuts facilitate the process of modifying specific settings.
4. The Presets setting is accessed by pressing the dialog pane. The dialog window allows for the modification of all parameters associated with a specific Preset. To modify the settings of a preset, click on the box and select the editing icon located next to the preset. Alternatively, you can access the preset's configuration options by clicking and holding the preset.
5. The Battery Life Indicator Icon is identical to the Front Screen Display.

More Tips:

To access the settings information, which includes the current mode, the time counter, the capturing setting, and the battery percentage, simply click on the Screen. To conceal them, click them once more. The setting information will be concealed upon the second press, enabling you to more clearly view your photographs to improve your composition.

To exit the Setting Menu, select a setting or press the Power / Mode Button or the Back Arrow.

To access the Dashboard and Preferences Menu, swipe down from the top of the screen. The interface is the initial screen that appears when you swipe down. To access the Preferences and Connections dialog window, swipe left from the right side of the screen.

As a Viewfinder:

The Rear Touch Screen simplifies the process of taking pictures and performing configurations. It also illustrates the appearance of your photographs with the chosen parameters. When you have completed the selection of your settings, simply touch the screen to conceal all icons and achieve a clean screen.

To compile your images, keep the Touch Screen on while recording and looking at the screen. If the Touch Screen goes off or sleeps while you are recording, you can either touch the screen or select the **Mode Button** or the **Power button** to wake it up. It is recommended that the **Screen Saver** be set to a duration of five minutes or more when filming a lengthy recording to prevent interruptions. The Touch Screen can also be configured to turn off after a specified amount of time (the settings can be found in the Preferences **Menu, Display, and Rear Screen Saver**).

View the composition on the screen when establishing mounted photos with the assistance of the Touch Screen. Allow the Touch Screen to slumber to minimize battery consumption after the mounting position has been established.

- **To preview photos and videos recorded**

The Touch Screen can be employed to evaluate your video and photo images following a recording session. The Touch Screen is equipped with the ability to identify whether you have captured a time-lapse sequence of images or burst photographs. Rather than sifting through hundreds of images from a Time Lapse sequence, the camera will compile them into a single file, which will facilitate playback. The sequence will be displayed as a distinct photo file on your computer.

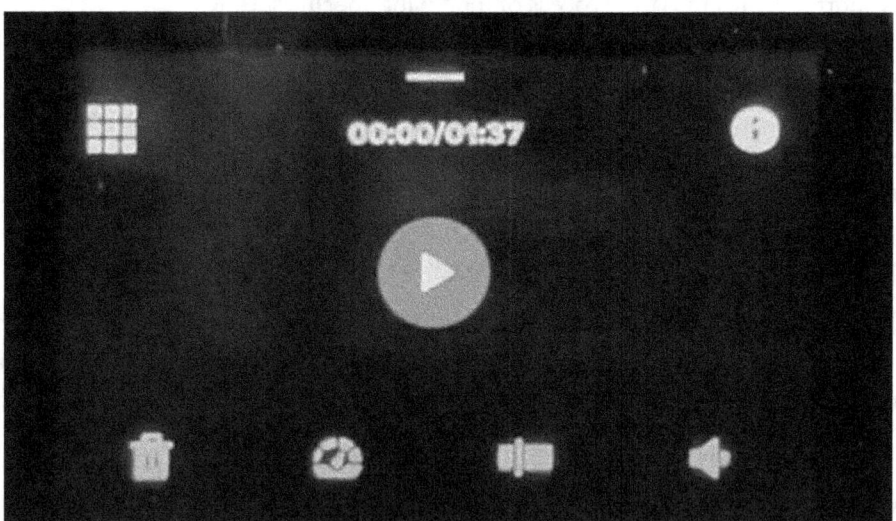

The media is displayed when the user swipes up from the bottom of the screen. The Touch Screen's playback elements are depicted in the image above. The icons can vary depending on the media genre being previewed.

Voice Control

Initially, voice controls can appear to be somewhat challenging; however, as you continue to experiment with them, you will realize their practicality, particularly when utilizing GoPro. In situations where one's hands are occupied; voice control provides a convenient method of controlling the camera with one's voice.

Recording and capturing photographs in a variety of contexts is achievable through the implementation of straightforward commands. Voice Control is more convenient than alternative methods for changing modes. Instead of navigating through modes by scrolling and swiping, you can immediately access your preferred mode.

To activate Voice Control,

- Swipe down the upper bar of the Touch Screen.

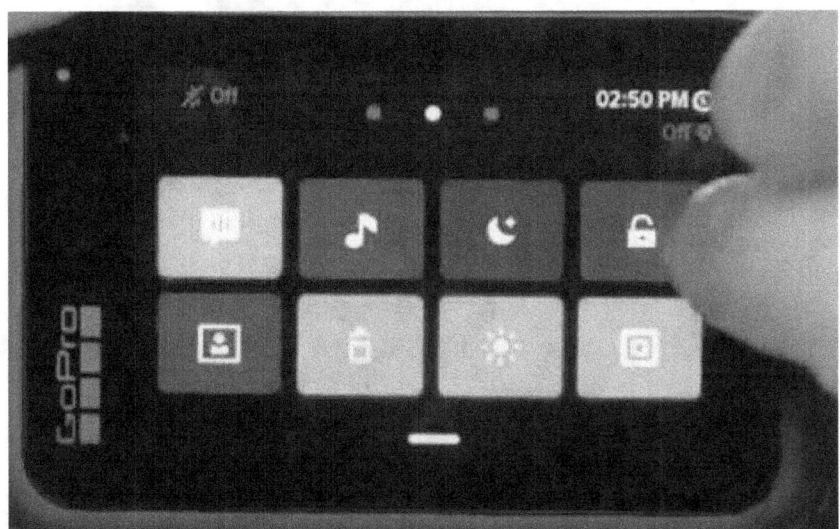

- Navigate **to Preferences** and click on it

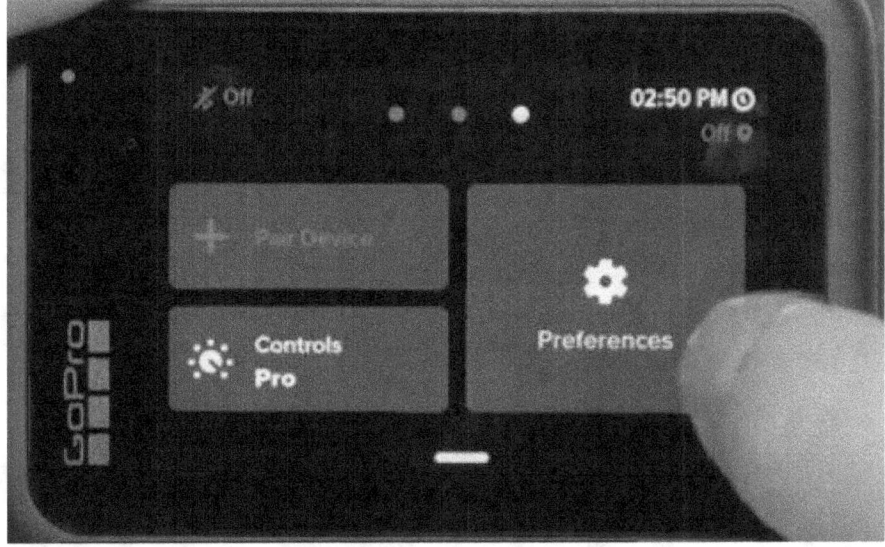

To eliminate the "x" by circumventing the blue icon,

- Scroll down to **Voice Control** and click on it

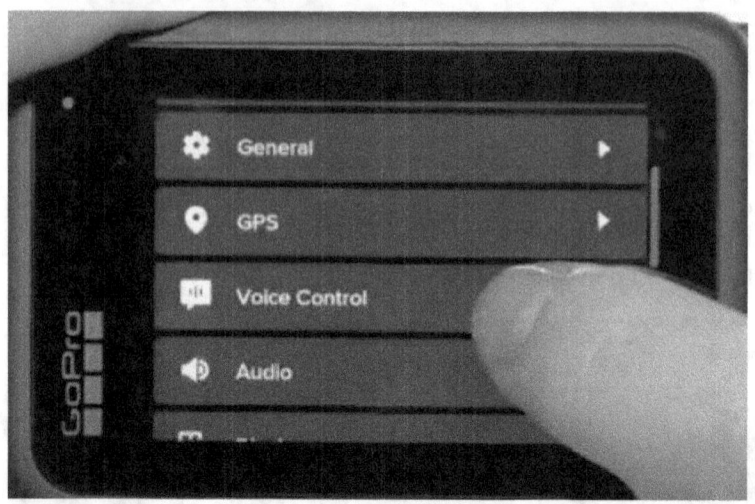

- Under the **Voice Control** menu, select **Language**

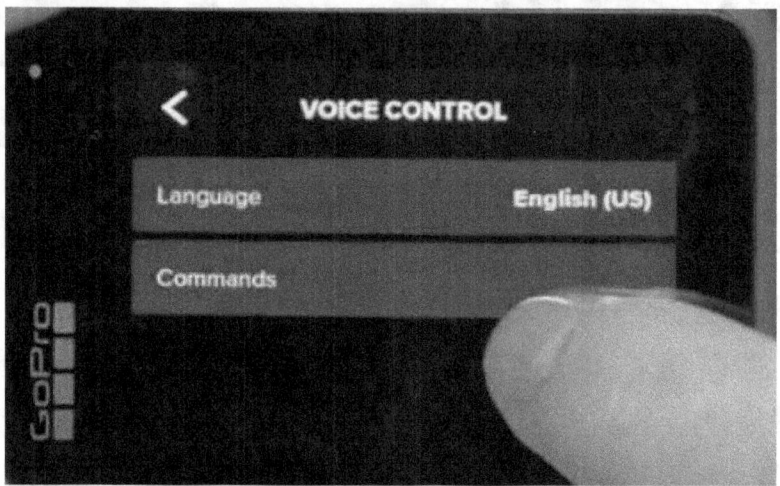

- In the **Language** menu, you can select any of the languages of your choice as displayed in the image below

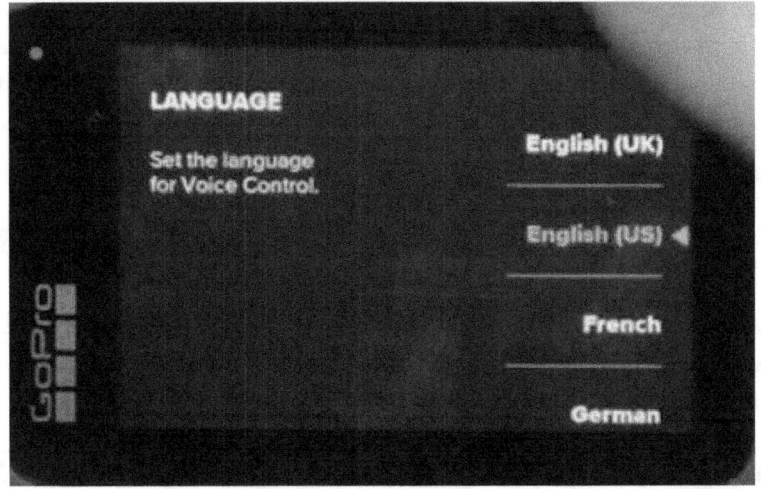

Despite its limitations, Voice Control is capable of achieving a great deal.

Here are a few commands that can be executed with your camera:

- **Capturing images or recordings in the current mode**

"GoPro Capture" (start recording or taking photographs)

"GoPro Stop Capture" (to terminate the recording of video in Time Lapse and Video Modes)

- **Instantaneously recording video or capturing still images by changing modes.**

"GoPro Start Recording" (to initiate video recording)

"GoPro Stop Recording" (to terminate the recording in Video Mode)

"When your camera is not in use, use the GoPro Take a Photo" feature.

"GoPro Start Time Lapse" (begins recording in Time Lapse Mode)

"GoPro Stop Time Lapse" (halts recording in Time Lapse Mode)

"GoPro HiLight" (to establish HiLight Tags in Video Mode, thereby capturing unforgettable moments).

- **Mode Switching Without Instantaneous Video Recording or Shot Taking**

"GoPro Video Mode"

"GoPro Photo Mode"

"Time Lapse Mode for GoPro"

"Deactivate GoPro"

Please be advised that there are instances in which the Voice Control will operate at its most efficient. They can also malfunction at times. For best performance, employ Voice Control when ambient disturbance is at a minimum. Before issuing a command, it is necessary to cease recording a Time Lapse or Video.

Ensure that the Hero 13 is not too far from you and that it can hear you clearly, particularly in areas with ambient commotion, such as the ocean or wind.

Additionally, Voice Control will not function when the microphone apertures are obstructed by water or sediment after being submerged in water or after being in the water. Ensure that the camera is shaken or that water is blown through the microphone openings.

WIFI/Bluetooth

A portmanteau of 2.4GHz and 5GHz Wi-Fi and Bluetooth is employed by the camera to establish a connection with mobile devices. The camera's Wi-Fi capabilities can be accessed without the necessity of being close to a Wi-Fi signal, as it is capable of emitting its signal. The Wi-Fi signal is not indicated by an icon or indicator light when it is active.

To access the Wireless Connections dialog,

- Swipe down the upper bar of the Touch Screen.

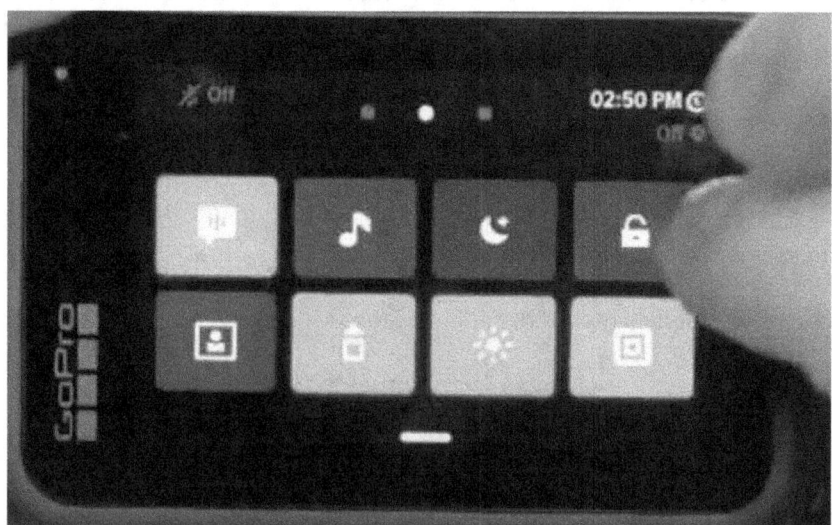

- Navigate **to Preferences** and click on it

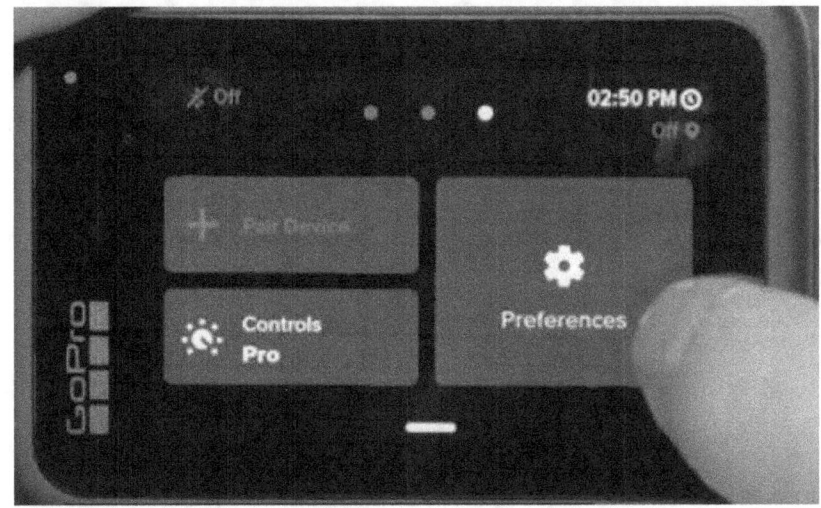

- Scroll down to **Wireless Connections** and click on it

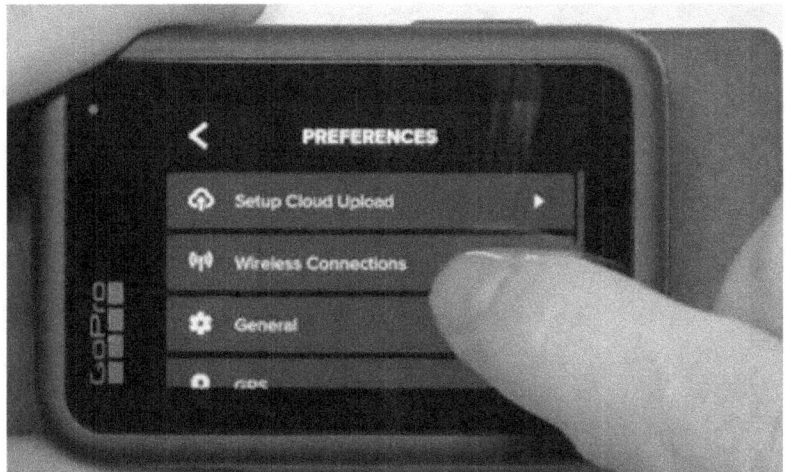

- In the Connection dialog box, you can select **Wi-Fi** or **Bluetooth** based on your preferences

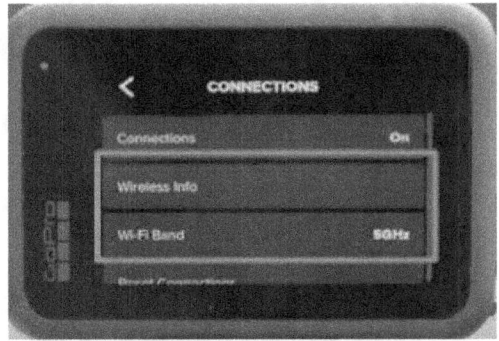

The Wi-Fi can be manually activated or deactivated, and the GoPro App (QUIK) can be connected.

To prevent excessive power consumption, the camera will automatically transition from Wi-Fi to Bluetooth. When it is anticipated that the camera will be inactive for an extended period, disable the Wi-Fi signal. The camera battery can be depleted if it is left on, as the battery consumption is negligible, approximately 3-5% over 12 hours.

CHAPTER THREE
The GoPro app and Sharing Contents

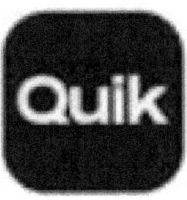

Quik, a GoPro application, is one of those applications that appears to possess an infinite number of features and tools, yet it also manages to render each one of them useful. The GoPro App is accessible on the App Store for iOS and the Google Play Store for Android. In other terms, your smartphone can function as a remote control for the camera.

The GoPro Quik App enables you to wirelessly upgrade the firmware of your camera. It is important to update the firmware of your camera, as this will provide it with the most up-to-date features and settings. Additionally, it is feasible to integrate video footage wirelessly. Your images and videos can be edited with the simple press of a single button. The applications enable the creation of videos on TikTok, Instagram, or YouTube.

By enrolling in the GoPro Subscription Plan, you will have complete access to all of the features of the Quik App. The GoPro Quik Subscription enables you to delete the SD card and continue recording without concern for losing your footage, as the app will seamlessly transmit your video to the cloud. The GoPro Quik Subscription provides unrestricted cloud backup and 100% fidelity on imported videos.

In addition, there are rumors that GoPro will implement AI technology to generate highlight reels of your video footage in the cloud, a new feature that will be available shortly.

Connecting your camera to the Quik the GoPro App
The GoPro Quik App is available for download on the Apple Store for iOS and the Google Play Store for Android. It is available for free download and use. After utilizing the account icon to log into your account, you will have complete access to Quik's features as a GoPro subscriber.

Open the application after it has been installed and select the camera icon located in the lower right quadrant. Subsequently, select the "+" icon or "**Add Camera**" in the upper right quadrant. Quik will assist you with the configuration procedure. Upon logging into the application, you must be aware of the necessary steps. The image and the identity of your camera will be displayed. If you possess multiple cameras, you can navigate between them by scrolling the screen.

After searching for your camera, Quik will indicate that it has been located on the camera's page. However, if the message **"Not Found"** appears beneath the camera's image, activate the camera to ensure that it is visible or discoverable. If it persists, verify that the Wi-Fi function of the camera is enabled in the **Connection Menu**.

Getting to know the App Properly

The control interface of the Hero 13 will be displayed by the GoPro Quik App once the camera has been wirelessly connected.

- **Live Stream**: It is employed for live broadcasting.
- **Media View:** This is the location where you can access, transfer, and modify media stored on the camera's memory card.
- **Cloud Auto Upload:** This is the location where you can upload your file to the cloud.

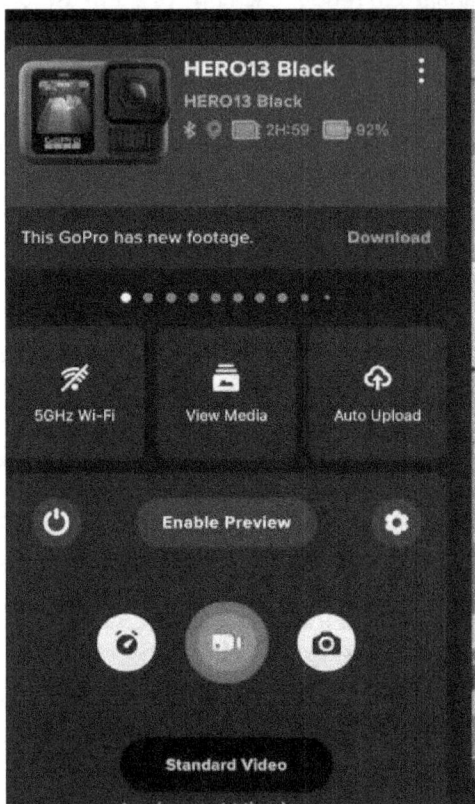

How to control the Quik App

With Quik, you are granted remote control over the Shutter Button, all settings, and modes of your Hero 13 at the bottom panel. We will now examine the application in greater detail. The control icons can be accessed on the first page of the camera controls, or the second configuration will be displayed in the diagram as illustrated below if you select "**Enable Preview**." Additionally, the scope will provide a view for capturing images. These icons will grant you remote access to the settings and modes of your camera on any of the pages.

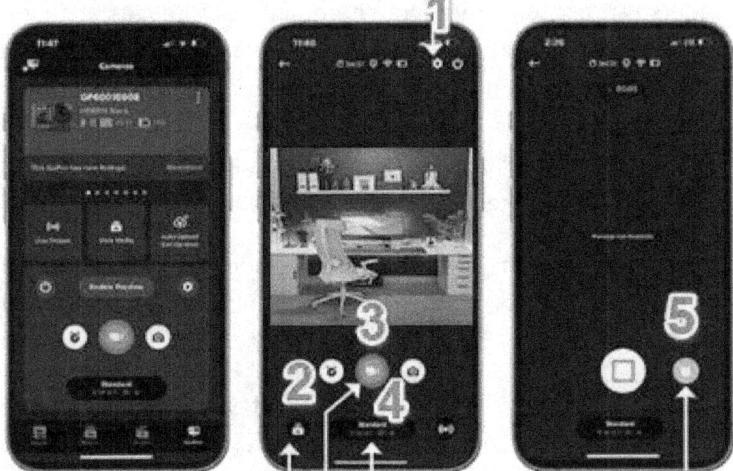

1. **Camera Preferences:** To modify the general parameters of the Hero 13, click on this icon. (General settings, including the ability to enable and disable Voice Control, Quik Capture, and Beeps).
2. **GoPro Media:** To view the video and images that are presently stored on the microSD card of your camera, click on this icon. Here, you can view, trim, extract, eliminate, or share them.
3. **Mode/Shutter Icon:** The modes can be toggled by swiping to the left or right. To initiate filming or photographing in the selected mode, press the **Shutter Icon**, also known as the **Circle Icon**.
4. **Preset Settings:** This section displays the Preset in which you are currently located, as well as its fundamental parameters. The preset can be modified or switched by clicking on this area.
5. **HiLight Tag (becomes visible when recording a video):** The HiLight Tag is an icon that indicates to the GoPro App where to highlight during editing. It is visible when a video is being recorded. Press the icon during the recording process to indicate the locations that you wish the app to emphasize.

After recording, you can view, crop, capture a picture, delete, and even download contents from the memory card in your camera. To proceed with the modification of clips and images with Quik, it is necessary to save the desired snippets and images to your device. When the footage is incompatible with your device, the GoPro App will automatically reduce the size of your recordings to ensure compatibility.

After concluding your use of the Quik App, you can disable your camera by selecting the **Power Icon** located in the upper right quadrant of the App screen. The application can be used to activate the camera if the Wi-Fi is still active.

GoPro Subscription

The GoPro subscription's advantages are readily apparent, and if you acquired your camera from GoPro's website, you can even receive an additional year at no cost. Owners of GoPro cameras should be cognizant of this subscription plan due to its potential advantages. Cloud storage, camera replacement, premium

Quik tools for editing, and mount discounts are among the four exceptionally beneficial features of GoPro's Subscription, which costs approximately $5 per month in the United States.

Initially, GoPro Subscribers can accumulate an infinite quantity of images and videos in their original, unaltered resolution on the company's cloud storage. However, the storage capacity is unlimited. By adhering to the setup instructions, it is possible to configure your Hero 13 to **automatically upload** all of your photos and videos to the cloud without requiring a connection to the app. This feature is extremely beneficial as it allows you to access your footage from any location and conserves storage space on your devices. However, larger files may require a lengthier upload time.

Furthermore, upon uploading your assets to the cloud, the cloud will generate an edited highlight video and archive it. When the highlight video is prepared for viewing, you will receive a notification on your mobile device.

Subsequently, it is imperative to consider the possibility of your camera malfunctioning during an expedition. In the event of a break or injury to your Hero 13 camera, you can replace it up to twice per year for a reduced cost in comparison to the original price.

Thirdly, upon subscribing, you will have complete access to the GoPro Quik App's editing capabilities and storage capacity.

Additionally, discounts are available for mounts. The majority of GoPro's mounts are available at a discounted price, which allows you to save some money. GoPro subscribers can view live broadcasts on the company's website. The GoPro subscription is not mandatory; however, it is recommended. It is impossible to overstate the advantages.

TIP: There are a few steps involved in offloading your files to a computer, a tablet, a phone, or GoPro's cloud storage after the recording has been completed

How to Automatically Transfer Files Using Wi-Fi 6

Wi-Fi 6 technology enhances the transmission of videos and photos from the GoPro Hero 13 to your devices. It is now simpler than ever to edit and share on-the-go content, thanks to the quicker and more reliable connections of this next-generation Wi-Fi standard.

Ensure Wi-Fi 6 Compatibility

Initially, verify that your router or mobile device is compatible with Wi-Fi 6. The Hero 13 is backward-compatible with previous versions of Wi-Fi; however, the most optimal performance and throughput will be achieved with Wi-Fi 6.

Connect your GoPro Hero 13 to Wi-Fi

- **Initial Setup:** The initial step is to activate the GoPro Hero 13 and navigate to the settings. Under the '**Connections**' tab, locate **Wi-Fi** and verify that it is enabled.

- **Pair GoPro App:** open the GoPro App on your phone or tablet and follow the in-app prompts to connect your device. You will now be required to establish a connection between your camera and your local Wi-Fi network.

Automatic File Transfer Setup

- **Automatic Startup Upload:** The GoPro App allows you to access the camera settings and configure the **'Auto Upload'** feature. Ensure that the Hero 13 is activated to initiate the automatic transfer of files when it detects a Wi-Fi connection.
- **Choose a Wi-Fi 6 network:** The camera is designed to automatically detect and establish a connection with any available Wi-Fi 6 network. If this does not occur, you need to manually select your Wi-Fi 6 network from the list of detected available networks on the GoPro.

Process of Transferring Files

- **Automatic Transfer:** The Hero 13 will automatically transmit new photos and videos to the GoPro App when it is either charging or turned on and within range of a Wi-Fi 6 network. It is notably beneficial for the transmission of large 5.3K video files, which can be carried out at a rate of up to 40% quicker than that of previous models when utilizing Wi-Fi 6.
- **Tracking Your Uploads:** The GoPro App will be able to directly display the upload progress of files within the app. It will notify you upon the completion of the transmission, allowing you to commence editing as soon as feasible.

Editing within the GoPro App

- **fast Edits:** Utilize the GoPro app's editing tool immediately after transferring files to perform a fast edit, trim, color correct, or even add audio.
- **Advanced Editing:** For more advanced editing, you can export your files directly from the app to a desktop or third-party editing software.

Sharing Your Content

- **Direct Sharing:** The GoPro App enables the seamless sharing of videos and photos to social media platforms, including Instagram, Facebook, and YouTube, with just a few touches after editing is complete.
- **Cloud Storage:** GoPro's cloud service subscription enables content to be automatically uploaded to the cloud, thereby freeing up storage on both your camera and device.

Color Correcting, Trimming, and Filtering Within-App

The GoPro Hero 13 is engineered to enable the seamless editing and sharing of your content. The GoPro Quik App, available on both iOS and Android, serves as the hub for post-capture editing. It offers a suite of features that can be used to improve footage directly from your mobile device.

Color Correction

Color correction is a critical component of video editing, as it guarantees that the footage has the appropriate color balance, contrast, and luminosity. You have a variety of alternatives to accomplish this within GoPro Quik, including:

- **Auto Color Correction:** This option automatically adjusts the color balance of your footage to reflect the intended scene of filming. It can adjust the saturation and contrast to enhance the visual appeal of the footage if it is too cold or toasty.
- **Manual Adjustments:** The Quik application provides manual settings for brightness, contrast, saturation, and warming, as well as exposure adjustment for those who prefer more control. You can adjust each setting to achieve the desired appearance, ranging from entirely natural tones to a slightly more stylized look.
- **Filters**: A variety of filters can be applied to videos to achieve any desired mood or effect. Filters also assist in color correction by emphasizing specific tones or reducing stark contrasts.

Trimming

Trimming is crucial to enhance the quality of your video content by eliminating superfluous segments and emphasizing the most significant moments:

- **In-app trimming:** GoPro Quik enables you to trim your footage with the utmost precision. The start and conclusion points of their clips can be readily determined by dragging the handles on the timeline. This is beneficial in situations where the recordings are excessively lengthy and brief snippets must be disseminated.
- **Highlight Tagging:** The Hero 13 offers Highlight Tagging through the Quik app, enabling you to quickly access the most noteworthy portions of your footage during the editing process. This feature simplifies the process of identifying and removing all the thrilling instances during the editing process.
- **Multi-Clip Editing:** Quik also provides multi-clip editing, which allows you to trim and subsequently combine multiple segments into a single, seamless video. This is the most effective method for creating montages or recounting the tales of your adventures.

Filtering

Filters are employed not only for color correction but also to incorporate creative effects into your footage:

- **Pre-set Filters:** The Quik application offers a variety of pre-set filters that can instantaneously alter the appearance and mood of your video. These modifications can encompass subtle alterations, the enhancement of the natural appearance of your footage, or dramatic effects that may lend it a cinematic quality.

- **Custom Filters:** If the pre-existing filters do not align with your vision, Quik enables you to generate a custom filter by modifying the intensity of the various effects. This allows you to establish a style that you can maintain in all of your videos.

Sharing Your Content

The GoPro Quik app simplifies the process of sharing your edited videos:

- **Direct Sharing:** The Quik application enables you to share edited videos directly on social media platforms such as Facebook, Instagram, and YouTube. This feature simplifies the process of ensuring that your content is presented to your audience as quickly as possible, thereby facilitating life.

- **Cloud Backup:** When you subscribe to GoPro's cloud service, your footage is automatically backed up the instant you modify it. In this manner, your original files will remain secure, and you will have the ability to access your edited content from any device.

- **Export Options:** The Quik app offers a variety of export options. Your video will be saved in a variety of formats and resolutions, as you may wish to share it in a location that necessitates a resolution that differs from the one that Quik typically exports. The app is equipped to accommodate a wide range of personal applications, as well as social platforms that have varying requirements for file size and format.

The Quik app, in conjunction with the GoPro Hero 13 Black, enables the user to access a robust set of editing and sharing tools that are ideal for on-the-go use. These features guarantee that your videos are refined and prepared for public release, regardless of whether you are a professional videographer or an adventure enthusiast.

How To Share Content Directly to Socials or Directly to the Cloud

The GoPro Hero 13 enables you to edit and share your content, whether you wish to post it directly to social media or back it up to the cloud.

Editing Your Content

GoPro Quik app and the camera itself are relatively straightforward to operate with the GoPro Hero 13's features:

- **In-Camera Editing:** The Hero 13 will allow you to perform minor edits, apply filters, trim videos, and perform light edits directly from the touchscreen. You will be able to rapidly compile a narrative using the footage that has been captured without the need to first transfer it.
- **GoPro Quik App:** The GoPro Quik app offers sophisticated editing capabilities, including automatic video creation, music synchronization, and transitions. This application is capable of editing the content of your smartphone or tablet when it is connected to your Hero 13 via Wi-Fi.

Share Directly to Social Media

The GoPro Hero 13 facilitates the seamless sharing of your GoPro footage on social media platforms.

- **GoPro Quik App:** Immediately following the editing process, you can share your content on social media platforms such as Facebook, Instagram, TikTok, or YouTube by utilizing the Quik application. The application will guide you through a seamless post-posting process to ensure that the most suitable content is submitted to the platform you intend to use.

- **Live Stream:** The Hero 13 camera supports live streaming directly to platforms such as Facebook and YouTube. This is accomplished by establishing a live transmission between the camera and the Quik application, which shares the user's escapade in real-time upon connection to a reliable internet connection.

Upload Content Directly to the Cloud

To ensure that you do not lose any of your memories, it is necessary to preserve your footage in the cloud. Hero 13 will simplify this process:

- **GoPro Subscription:** The GoPro subscription automatically uploads photos and videos from the Hero 13 to the GoPro cloud. This would take effect upon the connection of your camera to a Wi-Fi network and the completion of the charging process.
- **Auto Upload:** This feature simplifies the process. Auto-upload will commence the transmission of your files to the cloud when the camera detects a Wi-Fi connection. Subsequently, they will be accessible from any device that is logged into your GoPro account. This implies that your footage will never be lost, regardless of the circumstances surrounding your camera.
- **Access and modify from the Cloud:** Store your content in the cloud, and access and modify it through the GoPro Quik app or GoPro's website. It is possible to manage your footage using any available device and ensure that these moments can be shared or re-edited at any time due to their adaptability.

Tips to Share and Back Up Efficiently

- **Wi-Fi Connection:** Ensure that your Hero 13 is connected to a decent network to ensure that uploads to the cloud or direct to social media are seamless.

- **GoPro Quik App:** The Quik application is not solely for editing purposes; it also facilitates social media sharing. Additionally, Quik facilitates cloud storage management.
- **Check Cloud Storage:** Ensure that your GoPro subscription is active and that you do not have an insufficient amount of cloud storage, which could result in interrupted uploads.

CHAPTER FOUR
Understanding GoPro Hero 13 Camera Settings

Resolution and Frame Rate Options

Pro Controls:

Image Dimensions

The dimensions of the image (in pixels) for the various aspect ratios are as follows:

16:9

- **5.3K:** 5312 x 2988
- **4K:** 3840x2160
- **2.7K:** 2704 x 1520
- **1080p:** 1920x1080

4:3

- **4K:** 4000 x 3000
- **2.7K:** 2704 x 2028

8:7

- **5.3K:** 5312 x 4648
- **4K:** 3840x3360

9:16

- **4K:** 2160x3840
- **1080p:** 1080x1920

Video Mode Aspect Ratio settings:

16:9 Aspect Ratio info:

- **Zoom:**
    - Linear or Wide Digital Lens
    - A 2x zoom is available for 1080p (excluding 240fps) and a 1.4x zoom is available for resolutions of 2.7K and higher.
- **HyperSmooth options:** AutoBoost, On, Off (Off is not available with Linear + Horizon Leveling).
- **Variable Bit Rate:** The bit rate increases as the scene becomes more intricate and the recording becomes lengthier.

4:3 Aspect Ratio info:

- 2.7K resolution: 120/100/fps
- **Digital Lens Options:** Linear, Wide, Linear+Horizon Lock
- 1.4x zoom in both linear and wide modes
- **HyperSmooth options:** AutoBoost, On, Off
- **Bit Depth Options:** 8-Bit
- **Bit Rate Options:** Standard, High

- **Variable Bit Rate:** The bit rate increases as the scene becomes more intricate and the recording becomes lengthier.

5.3K, 4K, 1080p: Which resolution to use and when

Selecting the appropriate video resolution is essential for capturing footage that meets your requirements when employing the GoPro Hero 13. Each resolution—5.3K, 4K, and 1080p—provides distinct levels of quality, file size, and suitability for a variety of recording scenarios. The optimization of your shooting experience, whether you are documenting action sports, travel recordings, or ordinary moments, will be facilitated by an understanding of the advantages and disadvantages of each resolution.

1. **5.3K Resolution (5312 x 2988 pixels)**

The Hero 13 boasts an unparalleled level of clarity and detail, with a maximum resolution of 5.3K. It is recommended that you utilize it in the following circumstances and for the following reasons:

- **Best for Professional and High-Quality Content:** 5.3K resolution is the best choice for professional and high-quality content, as it produces images that are more detailed and sharper than those at lower resolutions, with nearly 16 million pixels per frame. It is the best choice for capturing high-quality footage that is intended for professional projects, including commercial video production, cinematic travel films, or documentaries. 5.3K is also suitable for footage that will be displayed on large displays, such as 4K TVs or theater installations, due to the additional pixels.
- **Optimal for Digital Zooming and Cropping:** The increased resolution enables greater adaptability during post-production. It is possible to apply digital magnification or crop the footage without experiencing a substantial reduction in definition. This is beneficial when it is necessary to reframe the image or isolate specific details from a wide-angle scene.
- **Use for Slow Motion at High Resolution:** The Hero 13 is capable of capturing fast-moving subjects with rich detail by shooting slow-motion videos at 120fps in 5.3K. This high frame rate enables the slowing down of the footage while preserving its precision and seamless motion.
- **Considerations:** The primary disadvantage of 5.3K is its file size. The footage requires a significant amount of storage, necessitating the use of high-capacity memory devices and an abundance of available space for editing. Furthermore, it necessitates an increased amount of processing capacity for modification and playback. Another factor to consider is the increased battery consumption, as recorded at 5.3K depletes the battery more rapidly than recording at lower resolutions.
- **When to Use:**
    - Recording high-detail sceneries, such as cityscapes or landscapes.
    - Creating cinematic videos that prioritize quality.
    - Capturing footage for commercial or professional editing purposes.
    - Developing content for large displays, such as 4K TVs.
    - Recording action sports or events that necessitate slow-motion footage.

2. 4K Resolution (3840 x 2160 pixels)

4K is a resolution that is widely used and effectively balances quality and practicality. It is extensively used in a variety of consumer electronics, such as TVs, monitors, and streaming services. To optimize the use of 4K on the GoPro Hero 13, follow these steps:

- **Best for High-Quality Videos with Manageable File Sizes:** The most suitable option for high-quality videos with manageable file sizes is to shoot in 4K, which offers a substantial improvement in detail compared to 1080p and is less processor and storage-intensive than 5.3K. The video quality is exceptional, rendering it appropriate for a wide range of professional applications, such as content creation, vlogging, and short films.
- **Smooth Slow Motion:** The Hero 13 is capable of capturing 4K video at a frame rate of up to 120fps, which enables the creation of fluid slow-motion effects. This feature is particularly beneficial for inventive transitions, sports, or action sequences in which slow motion enhances the impact of the footage.
- **Commonly Supported on Devices and Platforms:** 4K is a versatile resolution for general use, as it is extensively supported on modern TVs, smartphones, and streaming services. 4K guarantees that your footage remains interoperable with viewers' devices while maintaining high resolution for uploading to social media or YouTube.
- **Editing Flexibility without Resource Overload:** Although 4K necessitates more resources for editing than 1080p, it is significantly simpler to manage than 5.3K. This renders it an advantageous option for projects that necessitate high-quality images without necessitating the highest resolution possible.
- **Considerations:** Although 4K provides a good compromise between quality and file size, it still requires a substantial amount of storage space. Ensure that your memory device is capable of accommodating the data rate required for 4K, particularly at higher frame rates. Battery consumption is also greater than 1080p, but it is less than 5.3K.
- **When to Use:**
    - Developing videos for streaming platforms, YouTube, or social media.
    - Capturing slow-motion content with high-quality detail.
    - Recording travel footage or vlogging with a focus on quality.
    - Projects in which it is desirable to crop the footage without sacrificing a significant amount of detail.

3. 1080p Resolution (1920 x 1080 pixels)

The accepted standard for the majority of routine video recording tasks is 1080p. It strikes an appropriate equilibrium between battery life, file size, and quality:

- **Suitable for Casual Recording and Web Content:** 1080p is more than adequate for videos that will be primarily viewed on smartphones, tablets, or conventional HD displays. It is appropriate for capturing brief clips that you intend to share online, family events, or ordinary activities.
- **Lower Storage Requirements:** Videos captured at 1080p consume less memory card space than those captured at 4K or 5.3K, enabling you to record for extended periods. This renders it a viable

option for extended shootings or scenarios in which additional storage or power sources are unavailable.
- **Extended Battery Life:** The recording of video at 1080p requires less battery power, thereby extending the duration of your shooting session. This is advantageous during extended treks, travel, or other circumstances in which it is not feasible to recharge.
- **Smooth Playback and Simple Editing:** The editing of 1080p footage necessitates less potent hardware, which makes it simpler to work with on the majority of computers. Additionally, the playback is more fluid, particularly when employing antiquated devices.
- **Considerations:** Although 1080p is appropriate for numerous applications, it does not offer the same level of detail as 4K or 5.3K. 1080p cannot be the best option if you intend to display your footage on large screens or require the ability to crop during the editing process.
- **When to Use:**
    - Capturing family events, casual vlogs, or daily moments.
    - Photographing for social media platforms that will be primarily viewed on mobile devices.
    - Recording extended activities that are susceptible to battery life and storage issues.
    - Generating web content that is not required to be in ultra-high definition.

Practical Scenarios for Each Resolution

- **Adventure Sports (Surfing, Skiing, Skydiving):** Use 5.3K to ensure that you capture the most detail possible. The capture of fast-moving action in precise detail is facilitated by the higher resolution, while dramatic effects are facilitated by slow-motion modes.
- **Travel and Vlogging:** 4K is typically the best resolution for travel videos and vlogs. To facilitate the sharing and editing of professional-looking content, it strikes a balance between manageable file sizes and quality.
- **Extended Shooting (Events, Long Trips):** In situations where storage or battery life is restricted, 1080p is the most practical option. It enables you to film for extended periods and provides sufficient quality for casual viewers.

By comprehending the advantages and constraints of each resolution, you can select the most suitable option for your particular requirements, thereby guaranteeing the most optimal outcomes for your footage.

Frame rates explained: 24fps, 30fps, 60fps, 120fps

Understanding frame rates (fps, or frames per second) is essential for attaining the desired visual effect when recording video with the GoPro Hero 13. The overall appearance, feel, and motion of the footage are influenced by the specific characteristics of each frame rate, which render it appropriate for a variety of situations. 24fps, 30fps, 60fps, and 120fps are thoroughly examined in this section, along with the appropriate application of each.

1. **24 fps (Frames Per Second)**

- **Characteristics:** The 24fps frame rate has been the cinematic standard for decades and is still in use today. It is associated with a cinematic appearance because it depicts motion in a manner that is more "film-like" and lends a slightly softer, natural blur to moving objects.
- **When to Use:**
    - **Cinematic Videos:** 24fps is the best setting for any footage that is intended to emulate a traditional film or achieve a cinematic effect. It is frequently employed in short films, travel films, and any content that is intended to convey a narrative.
    - **Low-Light Conditions:** The delayed shutter speed of 24fps enables a greater amount of light to reach the sensor, which can result in improved performance in low-light conditions.

- **Considerations:** Although 24 frames per second is suitable for obtaining a film-like appearance, it cannot capture rapid action as smoothly as higher frame rates. If the subject is moving rapidly, motion blur can be apparent.

2. **30 fps (Frames Per Second)**
    - **Characteristics:** 30fps is the frame rate that is most frequently employed in online and television content, and it is frequently regarded as the "**standard**" for general video. It maintains a natural appearance while offering a slightly crisper motion appearance of 24fps.
    - **When to Use:**
        - **Everyday Videos and Vlogs:** It is an excellent option for casual videos, family footage, or everyday vlogs. The motion is more fluid than 24 frames per second without appearing unnatural.
        - **Web Content and Social Media:** 30fps is a viable option for videos that are intended for online sharing, as it is the default setting for numerous social media platforms and streaming platforms.
        - **Balanced Look for Mixed Content:** A practicable middle ground between cinematic and fluid motion is 30fps.
    - **Considerations:** Although it provides a more authentic appearance for standard videos, it cannot be the best choice for fast-paced action in comparison to higher frame rates such as 60fps or 120fps.

3. **60 fps (Frames Per Sound)**
    - **Characteristics:** The video appears noticeably smoother than 30fps because it captures motion with more detail and less distortion at 60fps. It is frequently employed in sports and fast-action footage, where fluidity in motion is crucial.
    - **When to Use:**
        - **Action and Sports Videos:** Capturing high-speed activities, such as bicycling, skiing, or any rapid movement, at 60fps results in a smoother motion that is more visually appealing.

- **Slow-Motion Editing:** Shooting at 60fps is an effective method for generating slow-motion effects that do not appear disjointed, particularly if you intend to slow down the footage during the editing process.
- **High-Quality Online Content:** 60fps is an excellent choice for the production of high-quality web content with seamless motion, as it is supported by a wide range of modern displays.
- **Considerations:** Shooting at 60 frames per second will result in larger file sizes than 30 or 24 frames per second, and it can deplete the camera's battery more rapidly.

4. **120 fps (Frames Per Sound)**
   - **Characteristics:** This frame rate is predominantly employed to produce slow-motion effects and depicts motion with exceptional smoothness. The footage captured at 120fps will appear four to five times slower than real life when viewed at a standard speed of 30fps or 24fps, resulting in dramatic slow-motion scenes.
   - **When to Use:**
     - **Dramatic Slow-Motion Effects:** 120fps is the best frame rate for capturing slow-motion footage of fast-moving subjects, such as water spills, extreme sports, or other high-speed action. It is frequently employed to emphasize particular occasions dramatically.
     - **Detailed Motion Analysis:** 120fps enables athletes to conduct a thorough analysis of their form or technique by allowing for a detailed evaluation of rapid movements during activities such as sports training.
     - **Creative Cinematic Shots:** By slowing down specific views, 120fps footage can produce a visually striking impact that adds a cinematic feel.
   - **Considerations:** Files that are recorded at 120 frames per second are considerably larger and necessitate additional storage space. Furthermore, the battery life can be reduced at a speedier rate than at lesser frame rates when shooting at this frame rate. It is also crucial to bear in mind that the effect of slowed-down footage must be observed during the editing process; otherwise, it can appear unnaturally seamless.

Practical Recommendations for Using Frame Rates

- **For Cinematic Videos:** To obtain a film-like quality in cinematic videos, be sure to use 24fps. It is ideal for content that is intended to evoke a cinematic experience and narrative.
- **For general use and vlogging:** maintain a frame rate of 30fps to achieve a natural appearance that is appropriate for the majority of scenarios, such as social media, daily vlogs, and general video content.
- **For Sports and Action:** Select 60fps to capture rapid motion with fluidity, making it ideal for filming sports, travel, and any action-packed footage.
- **For Slow Motion and Special Effects:** use 120fps for slow motion and special effects. It is ideal for highlighting motion in creative endeavors or sports.

By comprehending the distinctions between frame rates, you can select the best choice for each circumstance, guaranteeing that your footage appears precisely as you envision.

Low-light and HDR settings for enhanced performance in different environments

The GoPro Hero 13 is endowed with features that enhance the quality of video and photos in difficult lighting conditions, such as HDR (High Dynamic Range) settings and low-light conditions. We will examine how these features can be optimized to improve the quality of your footage in a variety of settings.

Low-Light Settings

In comparison to previous models, the GoPro Hero 13 is capable of capturing superior-quality footage in low-light conditions as a result of software improvements and configuration adjustments. Here are some tips for optimizing your camera's performance in low-light conditions:

1. **Use Low-Light Mode:**
    - The camera's Low-Light mode automatically modifies the frame rate following the available light. For example, the Hero 13 can automatically reduce the frame rate to 30fps to facilitate the transmission of more light to the sensor, thereby producing livelier footage, when filming at 60fps in a low-light environment.
    - **When to Use:** This setting is advantageous for indoor shooting, dusk shooting, or any situation in which light is restricted. It is particularly beneficial for capturing dimly lit venues or night scenes.
2. **Set Lower Frame Rates:**
    - Adjust the frame rate to 24fps or 30fps to optimize low-light performance. Lower frame rates enable a delayed shutter speed, which allows the sensor to accumulate light for a longer period, resulting in more detailed and livelier footage.
    - **Recommendation:** 24fps or 30fps for low-light environments where motion capture is not a priority, such as indoor photos or night landscapes.
3. **Modify the ISO settings:**
    - The camera's sensitivity to light is determined by ISO. In low-light conditions, the image will be brightened by increasing the ISO; however, this can also introduce additional noise (graininess).
    - **Settings:** To achieve a balance between image quality and luminance, set the ISO minimum and maximum to a range of 400 and 1600. In extremely dim environments, it is possible to increase the maximum ISO to 3200; however, it is important to note that this can result in grainier footage.
4. **Use Protune settings for Manual Control:**
    - Protune provides manual control over a variety of parameters, including white balance, ISO, and shutter speed.

- **Shutter Speed:** In low-light conditions, it is important to use a reduced shutter speed (e.g., 1/30 or 1/60) to enable more light to enter the camera. Although this can introduce some motion blur if the camera is portable, it can assist in brightening the footage.
- **White Balance:** Modify the white balance to accommodate the lighting conditions. Set the temperature of artificial lighting to approximately 3200K-4500K. Set the temperature to 4500K to 5500K for outdoor night scenes.

5. **Utilize an External Light Source:**
    - Add an external light to your illumination system, if feasible. Lighting accessories that are compatible with GoPro can assist in illuminating your subject and mitigating the graininess that is often associated with high ISO settings.

HDR Settings for Improved Dynamic Range

High Dynamic Range (HDR) is intended to enhance the quality of footage in environments with mixed lighting conditions, such as those that contain a blend of black shadows and brilliant highlights. Using HDR settings, it is possible to achieve a more uniformly exposed image by balancing these extremes.

1. **Activate the HDR mode for photographs:**
    - The Hero 13's HDR mode automatically combines multiple exposures to produce a single image with balanced highlights and shadows when shooting photographs. This function is especially beneficial for scenes that exhibit high contrast, such as backlit subjects, sunrises, or sunsets.
    - **When to Use:** HDR is recommended for the capture of still images that contain a combination of bright and dark areas. It can assist in enhancing the details of the shadowy areas and preventing the brilliant areas from appearing worn out.
2. **Limitations of HDR for Videos:**
    - The GoPro Hero 13 does not support HDR video recording, in contrast to certain other cameras. Nevertheless, it is possible to accomplish a comparable effect by manually adjusting parameters such as exposure compensation or utilizing video editing software in post-production.
    - **Manual Exposure Control:** Utilize the Protune parameters to manually adjust the exposure level in challenging illumination conditions. By reducing the exposure compensation, it is possible to prevent light areas from becoming overexposed.
3. **Combine Time Lapse with HDR:**
    - The camera can be configured to acquire HDR images at regular intervals when producing time-lapse videos. The HDR images can be stitched into a time-lapse video that maintains a balanced dynamic range throughout the sequence using editing software at a later time.

Practical Tips for Low-Light and HDR Shooting

- **Camera Stabilization:** To ensure the camera remains steady during both low-light and HDR shooting, it is recommended to use a tripod or a secure surface, as shorter shutter speeds can introduce blur.

- **Avoid the Overuse of High ISO:** Although increasing the ISO can assist in brightening low-light footage, it is important to consider the noise it introduces. To achieve the optimal equilibrium, experiment with various ISO ranges.
- **Utilize the GoPro App for Real-Time Adjustments:** The GoPro app enables you to evaluate your footage in real-time and make adjustments to settings, which is beneficial in rapidly changing environments.

By effectively utilizing and comprehending these parameters, you can substantially enhance your footage in low-light scenarios and sequences with difficult lighting contrasts.

How to Set Up 4k/60fps Video Recording

Follow these steps to configure your GoPro Hero 13 for 4K video recording at 60 frames per second:

1. To access the settings menu, activate the camera and swipe downward from the top.
2. To access the video mode's settings, simply tap the **video icon**. You will now observe a variety of video resolutions with varying frame rates.
3. Navigate down to select 4k resolution.
4. The frame rate will be requested after selecting 4K. Opt for a frame rate of 60 frames per second, as the captured motion will be more detailed and seamless. Upon playing it at a standard pace, you will experience a delightful slow-motion effect.
5. Additional settings that can be modified include:

    - **Lens Mode:** The options are Wide, Linear, or SuperView, depending on the desired field of view. Typically, either SuperView or WideView is suitable for action.
    - **Stabilization:** Particularly when photographing handheld or in a high-motion environment, ensure that HyperSmooth is enabled.
    - **Protune Settings:** This feature enables more sophisticated users to manually control settings such as ISO, white balance, and sharpness, thereby providing them with even more precise control over the final image.

Optimizing for Reduced Resolution

Shooting at lower resolutions, such as 1080p or 720p, is frequently advantageous for a variety of reasons, such as prolonging the duration of the recording, reducing the size of the file, and preserving battery life.

1. **Switch to 1080p/120fps or 720p/240fps:** Initially, choose either 1080p for Full HD or 720p for HD in the video settings, depending on your preference and intended use. Select either 120fps for moderate slo-mo or 240fps for severe slo-mo after selecting either 1080p for Full HD or 720p for HD.
2. **Use Appropriate Lens Mod:** Attach the Macro Lens Mod to capture detailed, intricate views up close, or the Ultra Vast Lens Mod to capture vast angular vistas.

3. **Adjust Battery Use:** By shooting at a reduced resolution, your battery life will be significantly extended. For better recording time during extended shoots, it is possible to film at lower resolutions, such as 1080p at either 30fps or 60fps.

Storage and Battery Life Management

Power consumption and storage requirements are increased when high-resolution shooting is combined with high frame rates, such as 4K/60fps. To effectively manage these resources, the subsequent recommendations will prove advantageous:

- **High Capacity MicroSD Cards:** A microSD card rated UHS-II or UHS-I V30 will guarantee that videos are recorded effortlessly and without any frame loss.
- **Extra Batteries:** It is advisable to have spare Enduro batteries fully charged in advance, as the rate of battery consumption increases with higher resolutions.
- **Power-Saving Mode:** If battery life is a concern, you can reduce the frame rate or resolution to conserve power. Furthermore, the battery life can be enhanced by deactivating features such as the front screen and GPS.

Post-Processing Considerations

With footage captured in 4K/60fps, there is ample opportunity for editing flexibility:

- **Slow-Motion Effects:** The higher frame rates can be employed to create some quite dramatic slow-motion effects without sacrificing fluidity.

- **Cropping and Stabilization:** High resolution enables you to compress or stabilize your footage without compromising quality, particularly if you have captured it in a wider field of view.

QuikCapture mode: Instant recording with a single button press

QuikCapture can activate the GoPro and autonomously record video or a time-lapse with a single button press. By default, this feature is activated. Time Lapse extended press is not supported by HERO13/12/11 Black cameras.

How to Use GoPro QuickCapture

There are a few strategies to employ when utilizing QuikCapture. The initial step is to activate the feature. It is enabled by default on certain models, while it is disabled by default on others. To verify or adjust it, navigate to

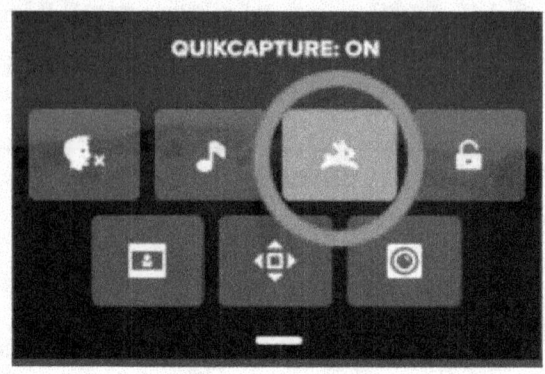

Preferences > QuikCapture > ON/OFF

(The menu settings are slightly different on older models of GoPros, but the concept is the same.)

Subsequently, you are restricted to the capture of time-lapse photographs or video. It is incompatible with other filming modes, such as time-lapse video or burst mode.

Thirdly, certain techniques are not inherently intuitive to utilize.

1. When the camera is turned off, pressing the shutter button located at the top (with the red circle) will activate it and commence video recording without the need to press any additional buttons. It retains the most recent video parameters that were employed and will revert to them.
2. To initiate the process of capturing time-lapse photographs, the shutter button is held down for three seconds, as opposed to being pressed. The camera will then promptly commence the capture of time-lapse photos upon powering up.
3. The final trick to be aware of is that the camera is not only turned off but the filmmaking is also halted when the shutter button is pressed again to cease the recording. Therefore, to perform any additional tasks, it will be necessary to reactivate the camera.

CHAPTER FIVE
LENS AND MODS

Introduction to Interchangeable Lenses and Mods

The GoPro Hero 13 introduces a new realm of creative opportunities for its users, thanks to its innovative HB-Series modular lenses and modifications. These devices have been engineered to enhance the capabilities of cameras, enabling the capture of a wide range of perspectives that result in professional-grade results without the need for complex configurations or cameras.

Getting Familiar with the New HB-Series Lenses

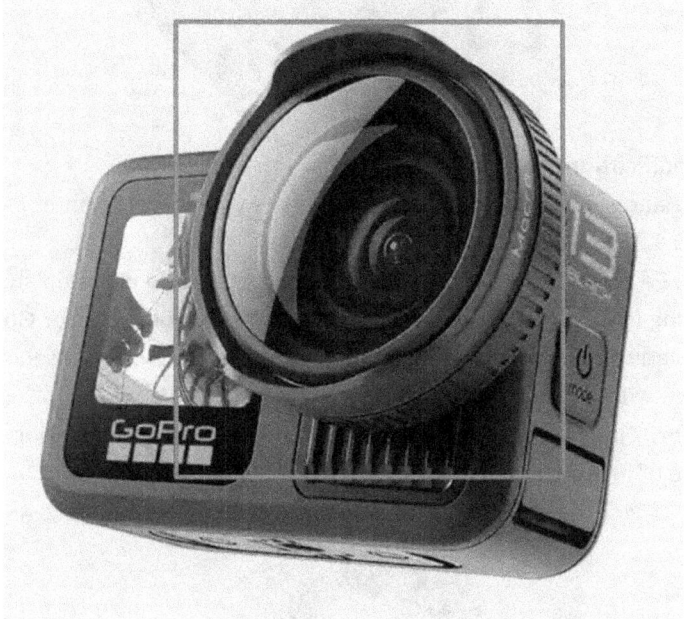

The GoPro ecosystem is revolutionized by the modular lenses of the HB-Series. Lenses can be interchanged to facilitate the capturing of an object. The camera's settings are automatically adjusted to facilitate seamless transitions by detecting the lens type.

- **Ultra Wide Lens Mod:**
    - **Field of View:** 177 degrees
    - **Aspect Ratio**: 1:1
    - **Special Feature:** The wide field of view of this lens mod is ideal for documenting expansive images, such as landscapes or action photos. Additionally, the HyperSmooth stabilization offered by GoPro is supported by this lens mod, even on the broadest images.
    - **Best For:** Landscapes, POV action, and situations where the utmost amount of space is required in the frame.

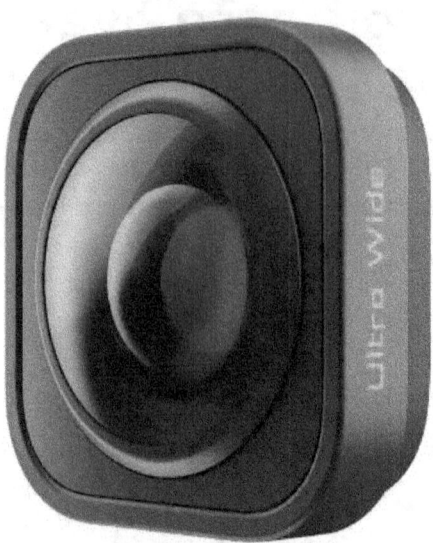

- **Macro lens Modification:**
    - **Focus Range:** The Macro Lens Mod enables you to focus on objects at a distance of as little as 4.3 inches [11 cm].
    - **Special Feature:** This lens is best for videography and close-up shooting. It is capable of achieving variable focus, a feature that is not available in other GoPro lenses. The lens is particularly well-suited for capturing small objects, such as insects or flowers, at a close distance with exceptional clarity.
    - **Best For**: Close-up shooting, nature shooting, and any situation that necessitates the capture of fine details.

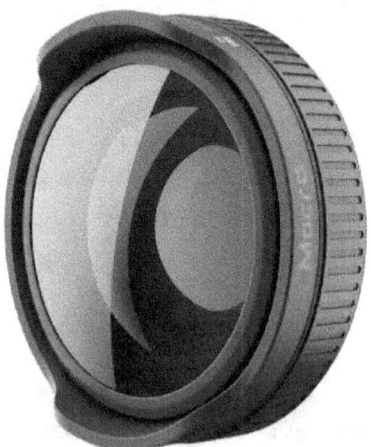

- **Anamorphic Lens Mod:**
    - Aspect ratio: 21:9
    - **Special Feature:** The lens will enhance the cinematic quality of your footage by exhibiting less distortion in ultra-wide images compared to conventional wide-angle lenses. It

provides in-camera "de-squeezing" and characteristic lens reflections, which facilitate editing.
  - **Best For:** Cinematic video production, wide-angle images with a dramatic impact.

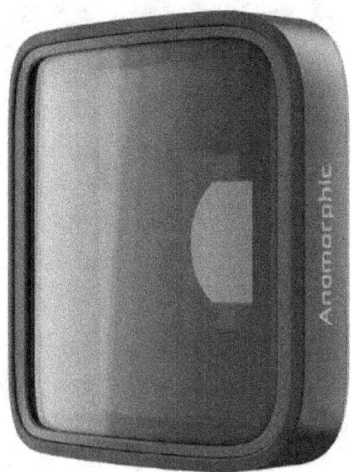

- **ND Filter 4-Pack:**
  - Filters that are included are ND4, ND8, ND16, and ND32.
  - **Special Feature:** Neutral density filters are best for obtaining motion blur for cinematic effects or shooting in bright conditions. The purpose of these filters is to enhance the control of exposure settings by reducing the quantity of light that enters the lens.
  - **Best For:** For professional video capture, motion blur effects creation, and bright light shooting.

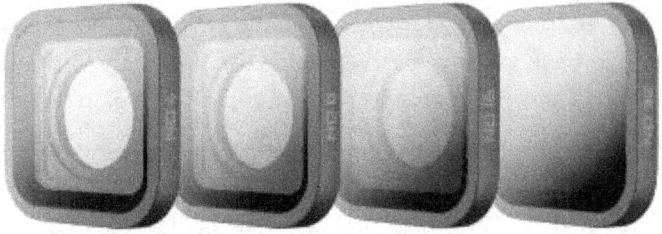

Snap and Go Magnetic Latch Mounting System

Furthermore, Hero 13 introduces a novel mounting method known as "**Snap and Go**" Magnetic Latch Mounting. It replaces the conventional mounting method of fasteners with a new mounting system that guarantees both speed and adaptability during installation. The magnetic clasp provides additional security for the camera while allowing for effortless adjustments to the camera's position or mount.

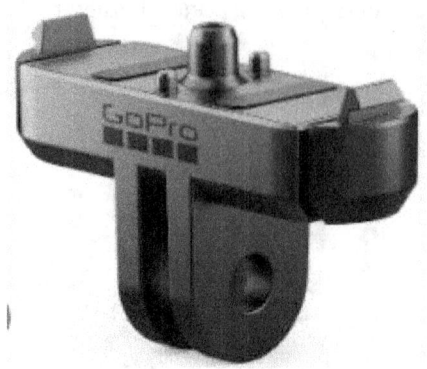

Why These Mods Matter

From interchangeable lenses to mods, the GoPro Hero 13 is a highly versatile tool that can be used to capture a wide range of shooting scenarios. Whether you are capturing breathtaking panoramic views of a landscape, extreme minute details in a close-up shot, or artistic frames of ultra-wide-angle cinematography, the modifications that these mods can make to your camera will precisely align with your creative vision.

The modular approach of Hero 13 enables a diverse spectrum of users, from professional filmmakers to adventurers and content creators, to accomplish high-quality results in a variety of shooting conditions and environments. Additionally, the Hero 13 is an effective option for expanding the limits of what is feasible with an action camera due to its advanced stabilization and class-leading video quality, which are seamlessly integrated with these modifications.

How to Shoot Using Ultra Wide, Macro, and Anamorphic Lens Mods

The GoPro Hero 13 is designed to be an incredibly adaptable action camera. The Ultra Wide, Macro, and Anamorphic Lens Mods have been introduced to enhance the versatility of that capability. Every one of these serves a distinct purpose and will enable you to accomplish a diverse range of creative outcomes.

Ultra-Wide Lens Mod

The Ultra-Wide Lens Mod provides a 177-degree field of view that is ideal for documenting action-packed scenes, immersive POVs, and wide-open landscapes. Additionally, this lens mod has introduced a new 1:1 aspect ratio, which allows for the cropping of footage into either a widescreen 16:9 or vertical 9:16 format without compromising quality. This feature provides greater flexibility in composing the shot.

Usage:

- **Lens Attachment:** The user must merely align the lens with the camera mount, and it will automatically secure in position. As a result, the GoPro Hero 13 automatically detects lenses and adjusts the parameters accordingly.

- **Best Settings:** This is most effective in outdoor environments where the user desires to capture the fullest view. It is excellent when used in conjunction with GoPro's HyperSmooth 360-degree Horizon Lock stabilization, which guarantees that your footage will remain precisely level and stable during even the most aggressive motion.
- **Best Scenes/Subjects:** Optimal for use in adventure sports, POV photos, and large crowd images, or when a panoramic view is required.

Macro Lens Mod

It is designed to capture extreme close-ups and has a minimum focusing distance of 4.3 inches or 11 cm. The Macro Lens Mod is best for capturing minute details in small subjects, including textures, insects, or flowers.

Using the Mod:

- **Lens Attachment:** Secure the macro lens by aligning the blue circles and then screwing it in. Additionally, it is equipped with an impermeable design, which allows for its use in a variety of environments without concern for the outcome.
- **Recommended Settings:** Your camera will automatically transition to an adjusted focus range once the Macro Lens is attached. Ensure that your subject is within this close focusing distance to achieve the highest quality images and video. This lens also supports slow-motion modes, which enable the capturing of detailed, high-frame-rate footage of microscopic subjects.
- **Best Use Cases:** Any situation in which high-quality imagery is required at a close range, including nature shooting and product close-ups.

Anamorphic Lens Mod

The Anamorphic Lens Mod allows for the viewing of a super-wide angle with the cinematic 21:9 aspect ratio, which is particularly useful when attempting to produce footage that closely resembles feature film footage. It is also intended to minimize distortion when attempting to capture wide-angle images. Additionally, it incorporates cinematic lens flares.

How to Use:

- **Lens Attachment:** The Anamorphic Lens Mod is automatically detected by the camera and is simply snapped into position, as with the other modifications. The Hero 13 then automatically reconfigures its settings to accommodate the lens and capture cinematic footage in high resolution.
- **Suggested Settings:** Best for shoots that aim to capture wide-angle perspectives with minimal distortion that is highly dramatic. This in-camera "de-squeezing" feature simplifies post-processing by automatically adjusting the footage to the appropriate aspect ratio.
- **Suitable for:** Filmmaking, documenting dramatic vistas, or any occasion that requires a cinematic atmosphere.

Tips to get the most out of your footage

- **Experiment with different angles:** Each lens mod provides distinct benefits; test out various perspectives and angles to discover how they can improve your photographs.
- **Utilize the GoPro App:** Utilize the GoPro app until you can observe the preview of a shot in real time. Occasionally, this can be quite beneficial when utilizing a Macro Lens Mod to guarantee that your subject is in precise focus.
- **Lighting:** The Macro and Anamorphic lenses require a significant quantity of light, which is crucial for these cameras. To ensure that the footage contains the utmost amount of detail, ensure that the subject is well-lit.

Attaching and Taking Off Mods

The new GoPro Hero 13 is engineered to provide a modular experience through the use of new HB-Series lens upgrades. The following is a method for the effective attachment and removal of modifications.

Attaching a Lens Mod

- To prevent any potential injury during the final stages of the procedure, the camera must initially be turned off.
- Align the Hero 13 lens mount with the ordered lens mod. Markers, such as blue circles, are present on both the lens adapter and the camera body to facilitate accurate alignment.
- Press the mod firmly onto the camera's lens mount until it snaps into position. If the lens mod clicks, it has been securely secured into position. Rotate it clockwise until it does. The mod is positioned in a position that is both impermeable and stable during use during that rotation.
- The GoPro Hero 13 automatically detects the sort of affixed lens mod after the attachment is complete. Consequently, the software will automatically modify the parameters to the most suitable configuration for the specific lens, whether it is the Ultra-Wide for wide photos or the Macro for close-ups.

Removing a Lens Mod

1. To prevent any potential issues with the lens or the camera, it is necessary to power off the camera before removing a lens mod.
2. Twist the lens mod counterclockwise while maintaining a firm grip. Release of the device from the lens mount would be achieved through this action.
3. Gently remove the adapter from the camera body after it has been unlocked. Ensure that the lens mod is enclosed in a case or container to prevent damage.

Things to Keep in Mind

- **Waterproof:** The waterproofing of the GoPro is a consideration in the design of each mod. Conversely, the lens adapter must be properly attached to prevent it from leaking during underwater shooting.
- **Handling and Care:** The bulbous front of the Macro Lens is particularly susceptible to abrasion, which is why the lens modifications require special handling and care. When the modifications are not in use, install lens covers and handle them with care.
- **Compatibility:** These lens modifications are exclusively compatible with the Hero 13 Black. Ensure that you have the appropriate modifications that are compatible with this model, as other GoPro models are unable to accommodate these new features.

Best Use of Each Lens Mod and Filter

The GoPro Hero 13 is equipped with a variety of lens mods and filters, each of which is specifically designed to enhance the camera's ability to capture the ideal picture in any situation. The best applications for each of these lens modifications and filters are detailed below:

Ultra-Wide Lens Mod

- **Field of View:** 177 degrees
- **Best Use:** The Ultra-Wide Lens Mod is most effective when used to capture expansive landscapes, dynamic action photos, or any situation in which the user wishes to capture as much of the environment as possible. It introduces a new 1:1 aspect ratio, which allows you to crop your footage to a widescreen 16:9 or vertical 9:16 without experiencing any significant loss. This lens mod also enhances the performance of GoPro's HyperSmooth stabilization, rendering it ideal for fast-paced activities such as mountain bicycling, skiing, or any other action sport that necessitates maintaining a steady image.
- **Why It's Special:** This lens mod optimizes HyperSmooth performance by providing 360-degree Horizon Lock stabilization at 4K60, ensuring that even the most extreme activity is captured in seamless footage.

Macro Lens Mod

- **Focus Distance:** As near as 4.3 inches (11 cm).
- **Best Use:** The Macro Lens Mod is intended for close-up shooting and videography, providing fine detail that can be overlooked by the standard GoPro lens. It is optimal for focusing on objects that are up to four times closer than the standard lens, as well as for small subjects such as insects or blossoms, and intricate textures.
- **Why It's Special:** The Macro Lens introduces a variable focus capability that enables manual adjustment of the focus distance. This feature is particularly beneficial in creative or experimental shooting, where precise control over the focal plane is required.

Anamorphic Lens Mod

- **Aspect ratio:** 21:9.

- **Best use:** The lens modification in question is intended for filmmakers and content developers who desire to imbue their films with a cinematic aesthetic. In comparison to conventional wide-angle lenses, the Anamorphic Lens Mod produces ultra-wide-angle images with reduced distortion. Furthermore, the 21:9 aspect ratio introduces numerous cinematic effects, rendering it ideal for documenting highly dramatic footage in a movie-style format. This is particularly beneficial during storytelling, as the widescreen format enhances the emotional depth and immersive visual experience of your scenes.

- **Added Value:** The lens enables the camera to deliver a cinematic appearance by "de-squeezing" in-camera, which facilitates posts by enabling creators to focus more on the art than the science.

ND Filter 4-Pack

- **Filters Included:** ND4, ND8, ND16, and ND32.
- **Best Use:** ND filters are most effective for controlling exposure in high-light environments. Cinematic motion blur will be achieved in your photographs due to their ability to regulate the amount of light that penetrates. This pack is extremely beneficial when capturing videos in broad daylight or when attempting to capture motion within the footage by filming at a slower shutter speed.
- **Unique reason:** Upon attachment, the Hero 13 automatically transitions to Auto Cinematic video mode, adjusting its parameters in real time to optimize its performance following the surrounding environment. It is beneficial to achieve professional-looking footage without the need for numerous manual adjustments to the camera settings.

CHAPTER SIX
Advanced Features of the GoPro Hero 13

An in-depth look at HyperSmooth 6.0 Stabilization and Horizon Lock

The GoPro Hero 13 is the most sophisticated video stabilization that GoPro has been able to implement to date. It introduces its most recent version, HyperSmooth 6.0, which includes a Horizon Lock mode enhancement to guarantee that casual and professional action footage is enhanced to an unprecedented degree.

HyperSmooth 6.0: Unbreakable Stability

GoPro's award-winning video stabilization has evolved into the next iteration, HyperSmooth 6.0. Although it established a solid foundation with its predecessors, it subsequently developed into a more robust and competent platform that could accommodate a wide range of features.

- **Improved Predictive Algorithm:** HyperSmooth 6.0 employs an enhanced predictive algorithm that is more effective in predicting movement, thereby ensuring that footage remains smooth even in the presence of rapid, erratic actions, such as mountain biking, skiing, or surfing. The algorithm mitigates the jarring sensation that is associated with these abrupt movements and tremors in action sports.
- **AutoBoost Feature:** The AutoBoost feature is the primary feature that distinguishes HyperSmooth 6.0. It autonomously modifies the stabilization rate following the intensity of the action. AutoBoost activates the utmost stabilization when making sharp maneuvers, ensuring that the image is not cropped beyond what is necessary. Such dynamic adjustments guarantee that the field of view is not compromised while the highest quality footage is delivered.
- **Low-Light Performance Smoothened:** This was also one of the challenges that HyperSmooth 6.0 had to address in comparison to the previous models. Stabilization would continue to be effective in producing clear, stable footage, regardless of whether the filming took place in typically dim environments or at dusk.

Horizon Lock: Maintaining Perfect Alignment

The Hero 13 has also been enhanced in the area of Horizon Lock, which is crucial for the preservation of the horizon's level during recording in the event of rotation or inclination.

- **360-Degree Horizon Lock:** The Hero 13 is equipped with a feature called Horizon Lock, which ensures that the horizon remains flawlessly level even when the camera rotates a full 360 degrees. This case is essential for capturing footage that must remain level, regardless of the camera's orientation, such as when it is affixed to a rotating object or during aerial filming.
- **Horizon Lock with Enhanced Integration:** Horizon Lock operates seamlessly with HyperSmooth 6.0, ensuring a dual layer of stability. Horizon Lock ensures that the horizon remains level, even during the most demanding actions, in contrast to HyperSmooth 6.0, which maintains the smoothness of the footage. This feature is particularly beneficial during activities such as

paragliding or snowboarding, in which the camera's orientation is subject to change on a minute basis.
- **High Compatibility of Resolution and Frame Rates:** Horizon Lock offers a wide range of compatibility with resolution and frame rates, including 5.3K at 60fps and 4K at 120fps. It can be employed in any filming scenario, from ultra-high-resolution cinematic imagery to fast-motion shots.

Applications

- **Action Sports:** The combination of HyperSmooth 6.0 and Horizon Lock ensures that your footage remains precisely aligned and stable, even in the most dynamic conditions, whether you are recording a downhill mountain bike ride or capturing a surfing session.
- **Vlogging and Cinematic Shots:** This feature will allow vloggers and filmmakers to capture professional-quality footage without the need for additional stabilization equipment, such as a gimbal. The professionalism is maintained by Horizon Lock, particularly during the content creation process, when precise framing is required.
- **Aerial and Underwater Shooting:** Horizon Lock, Advanced Stabilization, is a game-changer for filming in the air and underwater, where it can be challenging to maintain a constant horizon and seamless footage due to environmental factors such as wind or water currents.

Video Stabilization

It is effortless to produce high-quality films with a GoPro and record in nearly any environment. However, it can be beneficial to acquire the ability to stabilize the camera to eliminate the unsteady effect that could otherwise detract from the video. If you are interested in learning how to stabilize GoPro footage during and after production, there are specific methods that can be employed to reduce or eliminate shakiness.

In this section, we will examine the process of stabilizing your GoPro recordings at any moment during the production of the ideal video.

The process of Stabilizing footage during filming

During the production phase, there are numerous methods for stabilizing GoPro footage while filming.

Use the built-in GoPro stabilizer.

The built-in stabilization function can be activated or deactivated by filmmakers. Nevertheless, there are no additional options or methods to modify the level of stability. However, the outcomes are not consistently dependable, and the video can continue to be disjointed.

Other stabilization equipment

Furthermore, it is possible to acquire stabilizing devices to be employed in conjunction with your GoPro during the recording process. Examples of this equipment include:

- Tripods

- Monopods

- Chin Mounts and Mouthpieces

- Poles

Maintain a steady body posture

If you prefer not to acquire or manage stabilizing apparatus, you can also adjust your body position during the recording process to enhance stability. Avoid bending at any time and maintain an upright posture while recording, whenever possible. Maintaining an upright posture and an erect spine will result in a more stable film.

The head is the most stable body portion, so it is possible to keep the GoPro close to your face while recording.

Build your stabilization rig

Another option is to develop a distinctive stabilizing system for your GoPro camera. A modest system can be constructed as a straightforward DIY project using PVC tubing and other common components. Stabilization devices can ensure that your camera remains stable during recording, which is advantageous if you are in a situation where other equipment is ineffective or if you have difficulty standing upright.

How to stabilize GoPro video after recording

Choose the right editing software

It is imperative to identify the appropriate software to stabilize GoPro footage that has been captured. You have the option of employing the video stabilization tools in GoPro Studio or another program that is compatible with GoPro footage and cameras to edit your films. In addition to other functions that can help you achieve the best final output; the software can provide capabilities that are specifically intended for video stabilization.

With the appropriate video editing software, stabilization will be effortless and rapid, and you will have the freedom to continue altering and incorporating effects until you are satisfied with the outcome. Nevertheless, it is important to consider that footage that is exceedingly unstable can be more challenging to stabilize in post-production. In certain cases, stabilization can result in a reduction in video quality.

By bearing this in mind and comprehending the process of GoPro video stabilization, it is possible to eliminate jittery footage from your GoPro recordings and experience consistent quality. Whether you take precautions before filming to prevent shaky footage or eliminate it in post-production using dependable software, there are numerous methods to create top-notch GoPro recordings every time.

Horizon Lock

To enable Horizon Lock:

1. Navigate to the [**Preset**] section of your video and select [**Lens**] for a compatible resolution/frame rate combination.
    2. A selector will be visible to the right, allowing you to select [**Linear + Horizon Lock**].

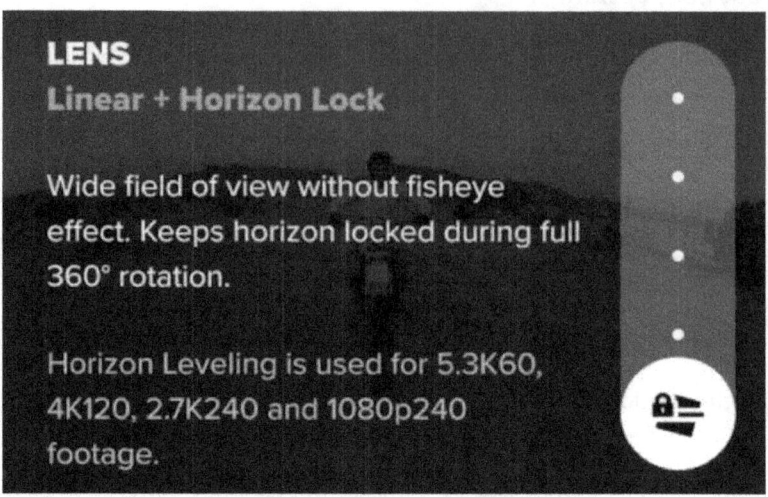

How to Lock Orientation on the GoPro HERO 13

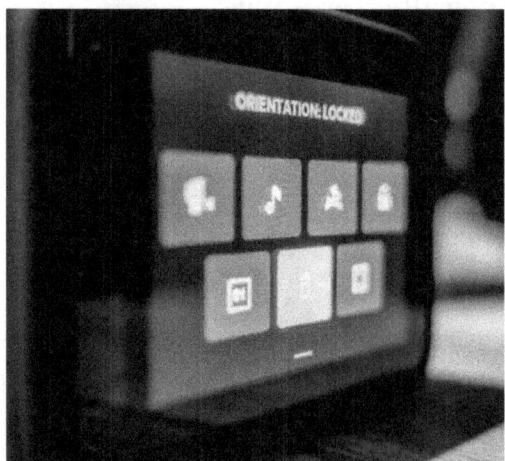

The GoPro HERO13 is equipped with sensors that can track the camera's rotation. Similar to your smartphone, it rotates the screen following whether you are holding it vertically or laterally. It is remarkable how frequently it is advantageous to mount the camera inverted. The image/video and screen will continue to be automatically rotated to the correct side by the camera.

Automatic rotation is enabled by default on the HERO13. Screen and filming orientation will rotate in tandem with the camera to ensure that the right side is facing upward.

Basic Orientation Lock

While the process of securing the orientation is straightforward and rapid, it is important to be cognizant of several functional details.

For basic use:

1. Access the dashboard's primary preferences. To accomplish this, swipe downward from the top of the screen. The dashboard is the interface that contains two panels of rounded icons.
2. Adjust the direction of your camera to capture the desired image.
3. Select the **Orientation symbol**. Located at the base, it is surrounded by a square and four triangle indicators. The horizontal orientation of the camera is indicated by the center of the lower row. If you are holding it vertically, it is located in the second row from the top, near the bottom right. The precise appearance of the symbol will be determined by whether or not Landscape Lock is enabled.

Unlocked resembles something like this:

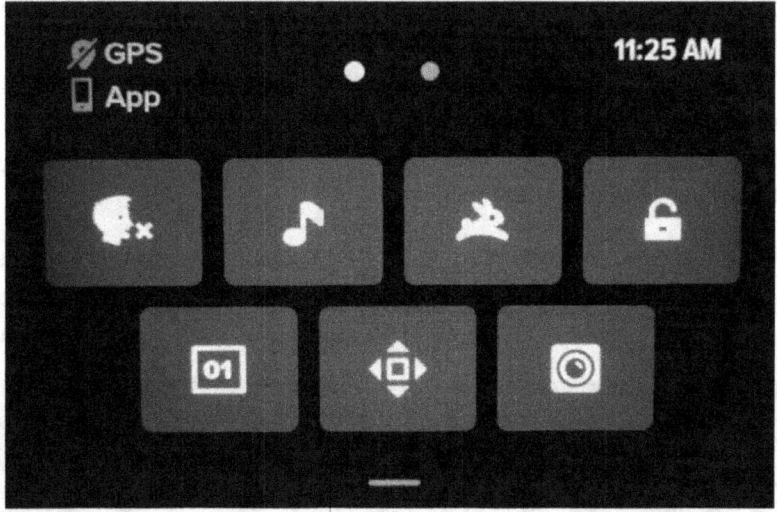

Locked like this with an arrow pointing in the direction of the orientation:

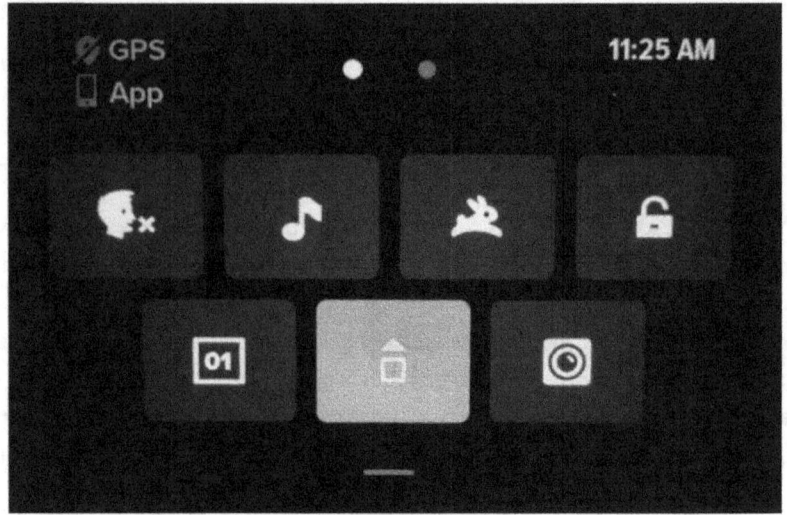

To remove the lock, simply press the same symbol again.

Enabling Landscape Lock on the HERO13

Furthermore, you can adopt a slightly different approach to problems, resulting in slightly different results. Utilize the **Landscape Orientation Lock** to accomplish this. Even though the overall operation is straightforward, there is one intriguing aspect that is worth comprehending. It can be accessed by navigating to **Preferences > Displays > Orientation**.

The orientation is not restricted by default on the HERO13. This is equivalent to the selection of "**All**" in this instance. Nevertheless, if you prefer to limit it exclusively to horizontal (**landscape**) orientation, you can do so.

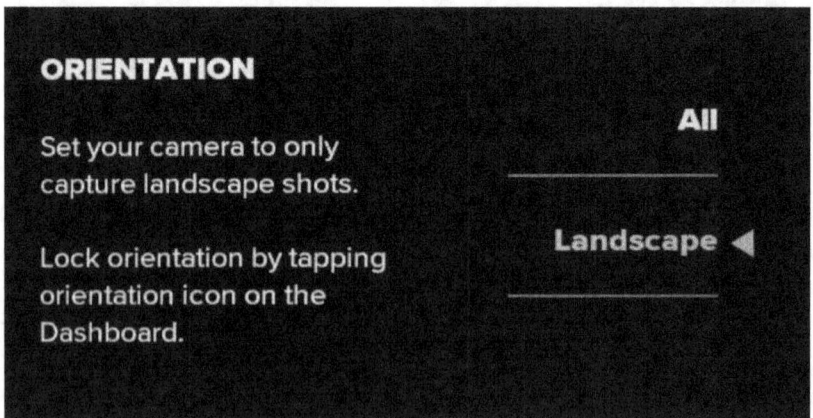

It is crucial to bear in mind that, even though it will only support landscape orientation, it is possible to rotate the camera to ensure that the menus and video footage are displayed correctly.

In other words, rotations of **90°** will not be permitted if the **Landscape Orientation Lock** is employed alone; however, rotations of **180°** will be permitted.

Nevertheless, it can be utilized in conjunction with the Orientation Lock icon on the dashboard screen if you only wish to shoot in landscape mode with the camera upside down or in landscape orientation with the camera angle right-side up.

When Automatic Rotation Detection can be Inconvenient

In general, the ability to rotate images automatically is beneficial when capturing them or viewing them on a screen. The capacity to fire vertically is a highly beneficial feature in specific circumstances. Regardless of whether you are documenting for TikTok or Instagram, vertical videos optimize the available screen space.

If you are filming for a platform that favors a more conventional horizontal (landscape) orientation, however, vertical video can be a nuisance. While it is feasible to rotate it in post-production, the process would be laborious and would almost certainly lead to truncation and compromised framing.

In general, the rotation is not a significant concern, as it can be readily rectified during post-production. It is relatively straightforward to accomplish this task with still photographs, and it remains so with videos.

The majority of video editing programs enable users to rotate videos by 90 or 180 degrees. Additionally, applications such as YouTube can be implemented to achieve this objective (under the Enhancement features). Once you have done so, there will be no discernible variations in the resolution or frame rate. Nevertheless, this is not always feasible, especially when you are attempting to navigate through numerous videos. And it introduces an additional item that must be addressed to resolve the issue.

Consequently, I would rather refrain from approaching it and capture it in the appropriate orientation. Utilizing a mobile phone for shooting simplifies the process, as how you hold the device will be evident. However, I have observed that it occurs more frequently when using a GoPro, primarily due to how GoPro users prefer to photograph. They are proficient in shooting while in motion, and there are numerous methods for attaching and managing the camera.

The issue is exacerbated by the potential latency that can arise as a result of the camera's delayed recognition of the orientation. The tempo is more sluggish than I would prefer, even though we have only been conversing for a few seconds. That can be a problem, as I have experienced on numerous occasions, as you can end up with a film that was captured at a different rotation than you intended.

Furthermore, the rotation cannot be edited until the video is halted after recording has commenced. The shutter trigger also functions as a landscape lock control for the duration of the recording. Therefore, the camera can transition to that mode if it detects that you are bouncing and that the image is now more vertical than horizontal. If the record icon is pressed without verifying, the vertical rotation will be fixed until the recording is terminated.

Therefore, to completely prevent this issue, I suggest you select the orientation.

Things worth Knowing

The rotation information is also included in the metadata of the image and video files, which instructs the playback application on how to display the image or play the video. As a result, the video can be played vertically (portrait orientation, or a rotation of 90° or 270°) or upside down (180° rotation) depending on the method of recording.

The rotation-locking option is classified as a convenience feature. The setting does not affect the principal image or video data. The metadata serves solely as an informative resource. Although I typically use the "Up" option (or "On") to capture videos, the capacity to secure the orientation is advantageous for editing, browsing, and viewing, as I rarely film in the portrait position. I am significantly more inclined to photograph in portrait orientation when using stills, which is why the auto-rotation does not affect me as much.

To interact with a variety of interface panels, the camera must be configured to landscape mode.

SELF-TIMER

In contrast to other features, the Self-Timer Retarder is available for all styles. Particularly, the Time Lapse, Photo, and Video modes. This will simplify the process of configuring the self-timer on your GoPro, as you will not be restricted in any way. A general strategy that is compatible with all modes is detailed below.

- Press the Mode button located on the left side until the Photo setting is displayed

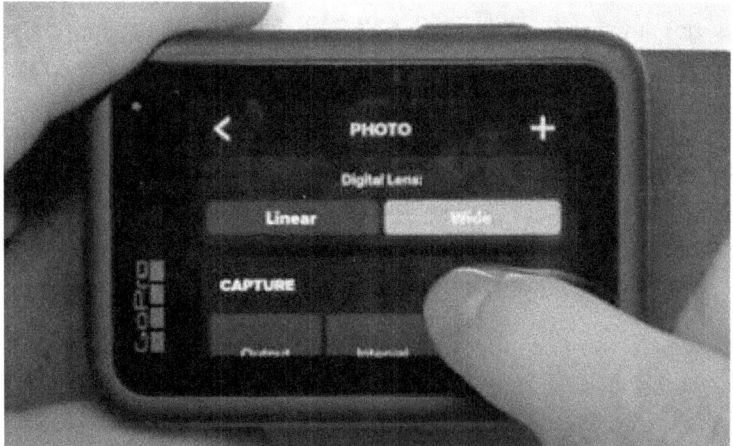

- Scroll down and click on the **Timer** option

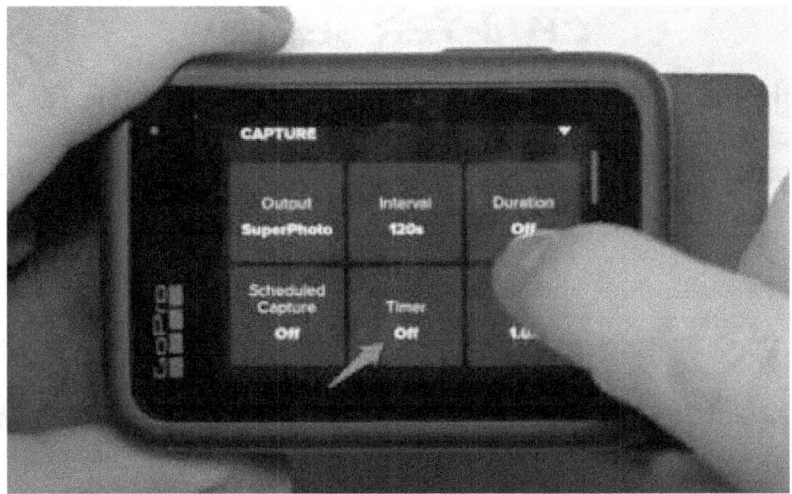

- In the Timer dialog box, Choose the **self-timer parameter**.
- Choose a timeframe that falls within the range of **three to ten seconds**.
- To initiate the countdown, simply click on the **Shutter** icon.

Note: By selecting the default Photo preset in the Photo mode, you can utilize a shortcut. The latter is indicated by a stopwatch symbol and is accessible on the left-hand screen. By selecting the latter, you can activate the self-timer for a duration of 3 to 10 seconds. You are required to press the red-circled shutter button located on the top of the camera once all necessary preparations have been completed. Immediately following this, the countdown to capture will commence.

CHAPTER SEVEN
EXPLORING PHOTOGRAPHY WITH HERO 13

Still Photography Options: Photo, Burst, and Live Burst Modes

In addition to their ability to capture high-quality videos, the GoPro Hero 13 provides a variety of flexible still photography options to meet a wider range of creative requirements. Hero 13 provides a variety of modes to capture the ideal picture, from a single moment to an action-packed sequence.

Photographic Mode

The GoPro Hero 13's photo mode is intended to capture high-resolution still images. The camera is capable of capturing images that are both detailed and crisp, even in challenging lighting conditions, due to its 27MP sensor. This camera preset is best for static photos, as it will capture the highest quality image. The HDR processing also assists in balancing exposures across an image, thereby enhancing the details in both the shadows and highlights.

Key Features:

- 27MP resolution
- HDR processing for balanced exposure
- Advanced noise reduction in low light
- Raw format support added post-processing flexibility

Steps to Capture a Photo:

1. Swipe your finger to the right side of the screen and click on the **Photo** mode

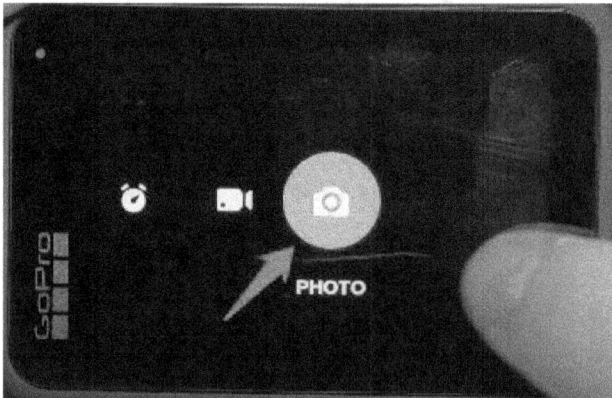

2. In the **CAPTURE** menu, you can adjust parameters such as HDR, Field of View, and Resolution. You can also modify the RAW format in this menu as well.

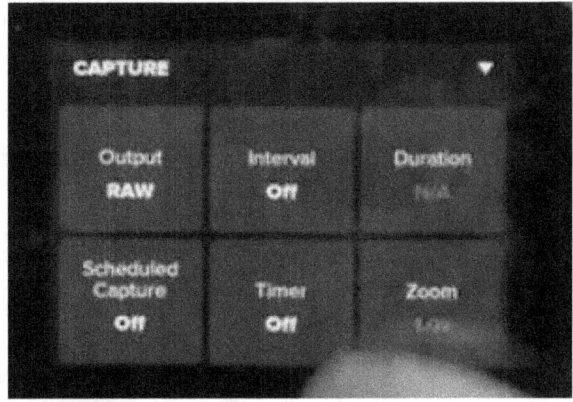

3. Utilize either the front or rear screen to compose your image.
4. Press the **shutter icon** located at the top of the screen to capture the image.

Burst Slo-Mo

This mode is best for capturing action that is in quick motion. The GoPro Hero 13 continuously captures a brief flurry of images to select the most suitable ones when it is activated. These modes are particularly beneficial in situations where the action is unpredictable, such as sports shooting or wildlife shooting.

Performance:
- A maximum of 30 images per second
- Best for Fast Action Sequences
- Burst Rates: 30 in 1 second, 10 in 1 second, etc.
- Utilizes GoPro's intelligent software to automatically select the best frame(s)

How to Take Burst Slo-Mo Photos:
1. Initially, it is necessary to activate the camera.
2. Tap the screen or press the **Mode button** continuously until you reach Burst mode, indicated by the icon displaying multiple images stacked on top of one another.
3. For instance, to establish a surge rate of 30/1 or 10/1, simply tap the surge icon. Select the best option for the action you intend to capture.
4. Aim the display at your subject to compose.
5. To capture the barrage, press and hold the shutter button. The camera promptly captures numerous photographs.

Live Burst Mode

The Live Burst mode captures a 3-second recording, with 1.5 seconds preceding and 1.5 seconds following the user's press of the shutter trigger. In this manner, the timing of the image capture will not be a factor, regardless of whether it is taken slightly early or late. This will be extremely beneficial when attempting to capture particularly dynamic images, such as a person leaping, a wave, or a sudden reaction, which necessitate precise timing. You can either retain the entire footage as a brief video or select the most suitable frame from the explosion at a later time.

How it Works:
- Captures 45 frames, including up to 30 frames from the moment the shutter is pressed and up to 15 frames after.
- Consider saving a single frame as a photo or the entire flurry as a brief video.
- 12MP images captured during the burst sequence
- Employed for the production of brief videos and photography

Steps to Capture a Live Burst:
1. Initially, activate the camera.
2. Continuously tap the Mode icon or the screen until Live Burst mode is reached. This configuration will result in an icon that resembles a burst, but with a play button, indicating that it fires a brief clip.
3. As a result, utilize the display to compose and frame your photo.
4. Select the "**Shutter**" icon. For a total of 45 frames, the camera records 1.5 seconds before and 1.5 seconds after the shutter is depressed.
5. After the frames have been captured, examine them and select the most suitable one, or retain the entire sequence as a brief video.

General Tips Applicable in All Modes:
- **Use QuikCapture:** By pressing the shutter button while the camera is in an off state, it is immediately activated and begins capturing in the most recently used mode.
- **Voice Control:** The Voice Control feature is activated by accessing the camera's settings. Consequently, it is possible to capture photographs without the need to contact anything by utilizing voice commands such as "**GoPro, take a photo**" or "**GoPro, burst mode.**"
- **Mounting and Stabilization:** Utilize GoPro mounting and in-camera HyperSmooth stabilization to capture the highest quality photos, particularly during action shots.

Shooting Close-up with the Macro Lens Mod

The Macro Lens Mod of the GoPro Hero 13 has the potential to revolutionize photography. The attachment allows for the capture of spectacular close-up photos with a distinctive, high level of detail that is not available in standard GoPro lenses.

Understanding the Macro Lens Mod

Thanks to its close-focusing capabilities, the GoPro Hero 13 Macro Lens Mod is engineered to enhance the most intricate details of your subject matter. It is equipped with a variable focus feature that enables you to focus on objects as close as 4.3 inches from the lens, which is approximately four times closer than a standard lens.

The most intimate vicinity facilitates the capture of intricate textures in detail, rendering it optimal for the close-up of insects, florals, or texture details.

Attaching the Macro Lens Mod

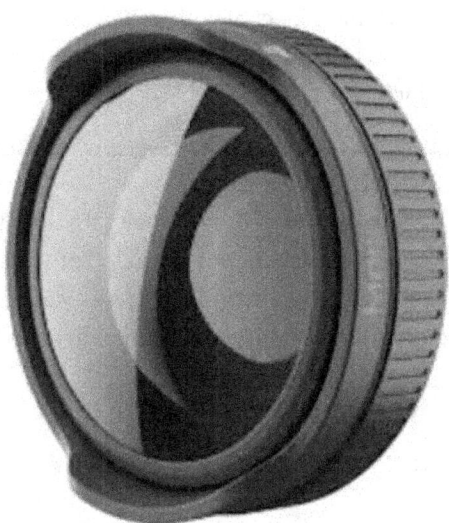

Attaching the Macro Lens Mod to your GoPro Hero 13 is a straightforward process, as this model features a magnetic latching system. Align the blue circles on the lens and the camera, and then rotate to securely secure the lens to the camera. The camera's robust and waterproof nature is preserved by this system, which maintains a watertight seal.

Optimizing Camera Settings

One of the most impressive features of the GoPro Hero 13 is its ability to autonomously identify when the Macro Lens Mod is activated. It will subsequently transition to mode, ensuring that HyperSmooth stabilization remains effective at these close ranges while optimizing image quality for macro photography by automatically transitioning to a lower resolution and frame rate.

The most optimum results should be achieved by utilizing the maximum resolution, up to 5.3K, and utilizing HDR settings to achieve better color and contrast. This camera's burst mode is an additional feature that is highly beneficial for macro shooting. It ensures that the highest level of sharpness is obtained by taking numerous photos in rapid succession.

Tips for Shooting Close-ups

- **Lighting:** Proficient lighting is essential for macro shooting. If necessary, an external source of illumination can be employed, although natural light is preferable. The camera's portability and diminutive size make it effortless to position the camera and light source precisely where they are needed.

- **Stability:** Even the slightest movement will result in a macro image with distortion. Consequently, it is imperative to maintain the camera's stability. Mount your camera on a tripod or position it on a stable surface. The GoPro's compact size allows for effortless installation in constrained areas, and it features a novel magnetic mounting system.
- **Composition:** The most captivating aspect of your subject can be the focus. This can be the texture of a leaf or the eye of an insect. The live camera view can be used to compose an ideal photo with the assistance of the 2.27-inch rear touchscreen.

Editing and Post-Processing

Upon capturing your photographs, the GoPro Hero 13 will facilitate their transmission to your smartphone or computer via Wi-Fi 6, which provides speedier connectivity. You can now employ editing software to further improve your macro photographs. While cropping refines your composition, making adjustments in the sharpness, contrast, and color balance settings will reveal even more detail.

How to Shoot HDR and 10-bit Color Photos

HDR and 10-bit color photos are captured by the GoPro Hero 13 Black, which provides superior detail, color depth, and image quality.

Understanding HDR and 10-bit Color

HDR Photography: HDR photography is the process of integrating multiple exposures to create a single image. This implies that the High Dynamic Range maintains equilibrium between the image's lightest and darkest regions. The photo will be more detailed in the shadows and highlights, without a washed-out sky or lost information in the dark sections.

10-bit color: Images are typically captured in 8-bit color, which can accommodate up to 16.7 million colors. The GoPro Hero 13 exceeds 1 billion colors when operating in 10-bit color mode. This expanded range results in more seamless transitions between shades, which enhances color fidelity and is ideal for portraying the lush greenery of forests or the drama of sunset.

How to Set Up Your GoPro Hero 13 to Shoot HDR and 10-bit Color Photos

Launch your Camera Settings:

- To access the primary interface, power on your GoPro Hero 13 and swipe down from the top.
- Select the '**Preference**' icon and then navigate to the '**Resolution & Frame Rate**' settings.

Enable 10-bit color

- A toggle option for 10-bit color will be available in the video setting menu. Enable this feature to ensure that the color depth of photos and videos is enhanced upon capture.

Activating HDR Mode:

- To activate HDR, navigate to the '**Photo**' mode settings. To access the '**Photo**' mode, swipe left; to access the preferences, touch the settings icon.
- The HDR toggle can be activated by tapping it in the '**Photo**' settings. The camera will automatically capture multiple exposures and integrate them to achieve the best possible dynamic range when a photo is taken in the future.

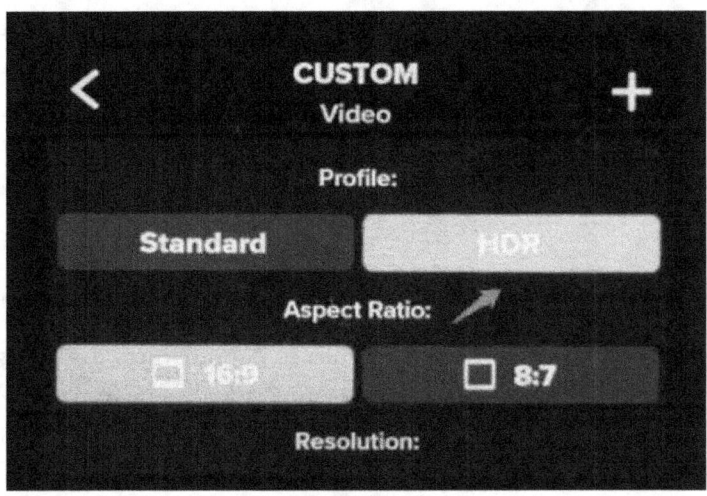

Tips for Shooting HDR and 10-bit Color Photos

- **Lighting:** HDR is the best choice for high-contrast settings, such as picturesque landscapes with brilliant skies and dark foregrounds. For better outcomes, photograph during the golden hour, which occurs in the early morning or late afternoon, when the lighting naturally emphasizes colors and contrasts.
- **Stability:** Maintain the stability of your GoPro to prevent multi-exposure distortion for HDR. It is advisable to utilize a tripod or securely mount your GoPro.
- **Framing:** The GoPro Hero 13 will have a wide field of view, which can substantially improve the framing of your primary subject, taking into account foreground and background elements.
- **Post Processing:** Although the HDR and 10-bit color are visually appealing straight from the camera, there is always the potential to elevate your photographs to the next level using post-processing software like Adobe Lightroom or Photoshop. These applications will have the ability to fully support 10-bit color editing, enabling you to easily make subtle adjustments to colors, exposure, and dynamic range.

Use Case Examples

- **Landscapes:** Capture the complete complexity and beauty of natural landscapes, from the brightest skies to the most intricate shadows in forests or mountains.
- **Urban Photography:** HDR can be employed to emphasize the minute details of cityscapes, as well as the brilliant highlights and profound shadows.

- **Action Shots:** The inclusion of a wider dynamic range and enhanced color reproduction renders even the most intense moments with vivid detail and clarity when photographing fast-moving subjects.

How to Shoot in Low Light and Night Modes

The GoPro Hero 13 is a highly capable shooting tool, particularly in the capture of elusive low-light scenarios, in addition to its designated niche in action videography. Learn how to optimize the use of your Hero 13 in low-light and night shooting by utilizing its advanced features to capture spectacular images when light is scarce or available in limited quantities.

Low-Light Challenges Explained

Noise, distortion caused by motion, and focusing issues are among the numerous drawbacks of low-light photography.

Most of these issues are resolved by the following important features of Hero 13 Black:

- **Advanced Sensor and Processor:** The Hero 13's camera features a 27MP sensor and the most recent GP3 processor, which further improves the clarity of images in low-light conditions. The sensor's larger pixel size will be able to capture a greater amount of light, resulting in an improvement in low-light detail and a noise reduction.
- **Night Mode:** This device is particularly well-suited for nighttime shooting, such as star trails or cityscapes, as it features a unique configuration that enables the capture of long-exposure photos.
- **Enhanced HDR and HLG:** The Hero 13 features Hybrid Log Gamma (HLG) HDR video and upscales photos to have a wider dynamic range, allowing for the retention of more details in the shadows and highlights when recording in high contrast conditions.

Setting Up Low-Light Photography

1. **Choose the Right Mode:**
   - **Night Photo Mode:** Utilize this mode to capture a long-exposure photograph. To capture clear images in low light conditions, it is imperative to employ this mode, which enables the shutter to allow for additional light to enter.
   - **Night Lapse Mode:** This mode is the most effective for capturing nighttime time-lapses, such as the movement of stars across the sky or the movement of clouds.
2. **Adjust the Shutter Speed:** Adjust the shutter speed manually, as low light conditions necessitate a reduced shutter speed. A reduced shutter speed, such as 2-30 seconds, enables the sensor to receive a greater amount of light, which is essential for capturing well-exposed and sharp night photos. Stability is essential for the camera; it is recommended to use a tripod to prevent the appearance of motion blur.
3. **Optimization of ISO Settings:** The ISO setting regulates the camera's sensitivity to light. Although a higher ISO, such as 1600 and above, can enhance the brightness of an image in low-light conditions, the likelihood of noise increases. The noise is mitigated by the advanced processing of

the Hero 13in this instance; however, it is always advisable to strike a balance between ISO and exposure duration to prevent the pixelated image.
4. **Use the Timer and Remote:** Use the GoPro remote or timer feature to prevent camera movement when striking the shutter button. It will ensure that your long-exposure photograph remains clear, and free of any superfluous camera motion blur.
5. **Enable RAW Capture:** Shooting in RAW format provides a significant amount of data compared to the standard in-camera JPEGs, which increases the flexibility of post-processing. This is especially beneficial in low-light situations, where subtle adjustments to exposure, contrast, and noise can significantly enhance the final image.

Night Mode Shooting Tips

1. **Find a Stable Position:** Consistently guarantee that your GoPro is securely mounted on a tripod or other stable platform. A lengthy exposure picture can be rendered entirely useless by a small amount of movement.
2. **Play with Exposure Settings:** The amount of ambient light can necessitate experimenting with exposure durations. For instance, star trails necessitate extended exposure times, such as 20-30 seconds, whereas cityscapes can necessitate an exposure time of only 5-10 seconds.
3. **Resort to External Lighting:** Occasionally, a slight increase in illumination around the subject can be beneficial. You may wish to incorporate an external LED light or GoPro's Light Mod to provide your subject with controlled illumination.
4. **Post-processing:** Enhance the quality of your nighttime photographs by employing post-processing software such as Adobe Lightroom or Photoshop. The exposure can be adjusted, noise can be diminished, and details that are concealed in the shadows can be revealed.

RAW mode for professional-level photo editing

The GoPro Hero 13 provides RAW photo capture, which enables users to achieve professional-level results when editing photographs. RAW mode offers photographers the ability to exercise more control over the editing process by providing unadulterated image files that retain a larger amount of data than standard JPEGs. The GoPro Hero 13 can be optimized for RAW photography by following these steps:

Benefits of Shooting in RAW Mode

1. **Increased Image Data:** In contrast to JPEGs, which compress the data and lose some details, RAW files retain all the image data acquired by the camera's sensor. This additional information is particularly beneficial for professional photographers who wish to optimize exposure, contrast, and color balance during the editing process.
2. **Improved Dynamic Range:** The ability to capture a broader dynamic range is facilitated by the use of RAW photography, which enables the recovery of details from shadows and highlights. This is especially advantageous when confronted with scenes that exhibit high contrast, such as a gloomy foreground and a brilliant sky.
3. **More Control in Post-Processing:**

- **White Balance Adjustments:** In contrast to JPEGs, which are pre-set, RAW files enable you to modify the white balance without compromising the quality of the image.
- **Exposure Corrections:** It is possible to make substantial exposure adjustments in post-processing without sacrificing quality, which is advantageous for underexposed or overexposed images.
- **Color Grading:** RAW photos provide a greater degree of flexibility in the process of color grading. You can adjust or improve the tones to align with your personal style or the desired aesthetic.

4. **Editing Software Compatibility:** RAW files are supported by the majority of professional photo editing software, including Adobe Lightroom, Adobe Photoshop, and Capture One. This facilitates a non-destructive editing process that preserves the original RAW data, thereby facilitating a seamless editing workflow.

When to Use Raw Mode

1. **Low-Light and Night Photography:** RAW files are best for low-light conditions due to their ability to capture a greater amount of information, which facilitates the reduction of noise and the illumination of shadows during post-production.
2. **High-Contrast Scenes:** RAW mode offers the necessary flexibility to balance the exposure and preserve details across the entire spectrum when photographing scenes with bright highlights and black shadows (e.g., sunsets, backlit subjects).
3. **Post-Processing Intensive Projects:** Shooting in RAW guarantees the highest quality for detailed work, whether you intend to make substantial adjustments to your photographs, such as heavy color grading, advanced retouching, or creating HDR images.

How to Shoot in RAW with the GoPro Hero 13

1. **Enable Protune Settings:** Navigate to the camera's settings and activate Protune. This will enable the selection of more sophisticated options, such as the capacity to select the file format for photographs.
2. **Choose RAW Format:** Navigate to the photo settings and select RAW as the file format. This feature will allow the camera to save images in both RAW (.gpr) and JPEG formats simultaneously, facilitating simple comparison and sharing.
3. **Use a High-Speed Memory Card:** A high-speed memory card (Class 10 or UHS-I/UHS-II) is recommended to efficiently manage the data and prevent latency, as RAW files are larger than JPEGs.

Considerations for Shooting in RAW

- **Storage Requirements:** It is important to ensure that your memory card has sufficient storage capacity, as RAW files consume more space. If you anticipate conducting an extensive amount of RAW photography, it is advisable to have several cards readily available.
- **Editing Time:** In comparison to JPEGs, RAW files necessitate post-processing to realize their maximum potential, increasing editing time.

- **Compatibility**: Ensure that your photo editing software supports GoPro's RAW format (.gpr), as some less common applications may not.

By capturing images in RAW, the GoPro Hero 13's sensor can be fully utilized, allowing for greater creative license and professional-level control over the editing process.

Live Streaming: Broadcasting directly to social media platforms from the camera

The GoPro Hero 13 enables users to broadcast in real-time from nearly any location, making live streaming directly to social media platforms both simple and effective. This feature is especially beneficial for athletes, vloggers, and content creators who wish to share their live experiences with their audience. The Hero 13 can be used to set up live broadcasting, and it is important to consider the following to ensure a successful broadcast.

How to Set Up Live Streaming on the GoPro Hero 13

1. **Connect to the GoPro Quik App:**
   - To live stream from the Hero 13, you must first connect the camera to the GoPro Quik app on your smartphone. For better performance, guarantee that both the camera and the application are updated to the most recent version.
   - The live streaming options can be accessed from the app's interface once you have established a connection.
2. **Choose Your Streaming Platform:**

   - The GoPro Quik app facilitates live streaming to a variety of platforms, such as Twitch, YouTube, and Facebook. The RTMP (Real-Time Messaging Protocol) feature is also available for custom streaming destinations, enabling you to broadcast to platforms that accept RTMP input.
   - **Facebook:** You have the option to go live on your timeline, a page you administer, or a Facebook group when broadcasting to Facebook.
   - **YouTube:** Ensure that your channel is verified and that live streaming is enabled in your account preferences to broadcast on YouTube.
   - **Twitch:** Twitch is an excellent choice for content related to gaming or action sports. To commence broadcasting, you will be required to opt into your Twitch account using the GoPro Quik app.
3. **Configure the stream settings:**
   - The Hero 13 is capable of streaming at resolutions of 1080p and 720p. Select the resolution following the intended transmission quality and the available network bandwidth. 1080p will provide superior quality if you have a robust internet connection, while 720p is a more secure choice for less robust networks.

- Additionally, you can establish the frame rate (which is typically 30fps for live feeds) and activate features such as HyperSmooth stabilization to guarantee that the broadcast is uninterrupted.

4. **Start Streaming:**
    - The live stream can be initiated directly from the app after selecting your platform and configuring the parameters. The camera will display a live-streaming emblem on its screen to indicate that it is currently disseminating.
    - The GoPro Quik app enables real-time interaction with your viewers by monitoring the video feed and remarks during the broadcasting process.

Tips for a Better Live Streaming Experience

1. **Stable Internet Connection:** A stable internet connection, such as a 4G/5G cellular connection or a robust Wi-Fi network, is necessary for live streaming. Before commencing the broadcast, verify that your signal strength is sufficient to prevent interruptions or quality degradation.
2. **Battery and Power Management:** The camera's battery can be rapidly depleted by live broadcasting. For extended broadcasts, it is recommended to either attach the camera to an external power source or use a completely charged battery. While in operation, the GoPro Hero 13 is capable of charging, which enables the broadcast to be sustained without concern for power fluctuations.
3. **Use External Audio for Improved Sound Quality:** The Hero 13's built-in microphones are satisfactory for general use; however, audio clarity can be enhanced, particularly in chaotic environments, by employing an external microphone. Via an adapter, the camera accommodates compatible external microphones.

4. **Optimize Camera Settings for Various Environments:** Modify parameters such as white balance and exposure to correspond with the illumination conditions. If there is a significant amount of movement, it is recommended to employ higher frame rates for outdoor streaming. To mitigate pollution in indoor environments, it can be advantageous to decrease the ISO.
5. **Interact with Your Audience:** Respond to queries or suggestions in real-time and engage with viewers by monitoring the comments. This enhances the engagement of your audience and provides a personal element to your stream.

Using RTMP for Custom Streaming

The RTMP option is available for platforms that are not explicitly supported by the GoPro Quik app:

- **RTMP URL and Stream Key:** Acquire the RTMP URL and stream key from the streaming platform you plan to utilize. In the live streaming settings of the GoPro Quik app, input the following information.
- **Custom Platforms:** This feature enables you to stream to custom destinations, such as a private server or streaming service that accepts RTMP inputs, providing you with the flexibility necessary for niche platforms or corporate events.

Practical Scenarios for Live Streaming with the Hero 13

- **Action Sports and Outdoor Activities:** Record live footage of skiing, sailing, or mountain bicycling. The Hero 13's HyperSmooth stabilization guarantees that footage remains constant, and its waterproofing to 33 feet renders it an ideal choice for water-based sports.
- **Vlogging and Travel Broadcasting:** Directly share experiences from various locations worldwide. The camera is effortless to transport due to its compact design, and it includes voice control capabilities that enable users to operate it without their hands.
- **Events and Performances:** Directly broadcast concerts, live performances, or public events to your audience. The audio quality can be substantially enhanced by the use of an external microphone, rendering it suitable for professional streaming installations.

The GoPro Hero 13's live streaming capabilities enhance the camera's adaptability, transforming it from an action camera into a live broadcast tool. With the appropriate setup and configuration, it is possible to provide high-quality live broadcasts that maintain the attention and enjoyment of your audience.

CHAPTER EIGHT
ADVANCED FEATURES AND SETTINGS

Checking Out GPS and Performance Data with Stickers

The GoPro Hero 13 expands the boundaries of documenting, witnessing, and sharing experiences by incorporating several advanced features. There is an option to visually represent performance data and GPS tracking through customizable performance decals, among other features.

This is the mechanism by which they operate and the most effective approach to capitalize on it.

GPS and Performance Data Tracking

The GoPro Hero 13 Black, like its predecessor, is equipped with a built-in GPS device that monitors your location, speed, altitude, and other performance metrics. It is of paramount importance to any outdoor enthusiast, athlete, or individual who wishes to enhance the context of the footage captured. The GoPro's GPS capabilities extend beyond the mere capture of visuals during an adventure; they also document the specifics of your voyage, including cycling, skydiving, or skiing down a mountain.

Working with Performance Stickers

An engaging and informative method of overlaying your GPS data onto your video footage is the use of performance badges. The variety of options that can be displayed within these decals includes, but is not limited to:

- **Speed:** Displays your current speed in real-time.
- **Altitude:** This indicates the elevation above sea level.
- **G-Force:** The gravitational force that is exerted as a result of acceleration.
- **Path:** To ensure that your path is visible on the map.
- **Lap Timer:** Capture the duration of each lap, including the time spent racing or engaging in circuit activities.

These decals are effortless to apply and personalize for video viewing, and they can be incorporated into your photo or video using the GoPro Quik app.

How to Turn On GPS and Use Stickers

GPS must be enabled in your GoPro Hero 13 to activate performance decals and GPS.

1. After activating your GoPro, navigate to the Settings menu by scrolling downward.
2. Select the "**Preferences**" option.
3. Navigate to "Regional" and select "GPS." It should be enabled.

After capturing the footage, transfer it to the GoPro Quik app.

The process for incorporating performance badges is as follows:

- Employ the Quik app to access your footage.
- Choose the video to which you wish to apply labels.
- Select the categories of decals you wish to overlay onto your video by tapping the "Stickers" icon.
- Adjust the sticker's size and position to meet the video's specifications. You have the freedom to include an unlimited number of decals and customize them to your liking.

Performance Sticker Benefits

A professional appearance will be achieved by incorporating performance decals into your GoPro Hero 13 footage. Additionally, this will enhance the elaboration and interest of your videos for your audience. These badges are brimming with valuable information about your activities, whether you are sharing a form of adventure on social media or evaluating your performance. They can also be beneficial for athletes to monitor their performance and enhance it based on data.

Sharing and Analyzing Your Data

The Quik application makes it effortless to share your video on various platforms immediately after you have edited it with performance stamps. The data that has been incorporated into your video provides the viewer with a more detailed understanding of the intensity and specifics of your activities.

How to Create Custom Presets Based on Environment

Using custom presets, it is effortless to transition between the optimal parameters for various filming conditions, resulting in high-quality footage.

Understanding Key Settings

It is crucial to comprehend the primary parameters that must be modified before developing these personalized presets.

Resolution and Frame Rate:

- **Resolution:** The grade of the video that is to be captured. The resolutions available are 5.3K, 4K, 2.7K, and 1080p.
- **Frame Rate:** The greatest rates, such as 120fps, are intended for slow motion, while normal rates, such as 30fps, should be suitable for regular video.
- **Field of View:** Wide, SuperView, Linear, and Narrow are the available options. The field of view (FOV) is the region of the scene that is captured. A wider field of view is advantageous for actions, while a narrower view guarantees optimal concentration on a subject.
- **HyperSmooth Stabilization:** It is particularly beneficial in cycling and running, as it reduces the amount of jolting in the footage.
- **White Balance:** Adjust this setting to ensure that the color is accurate. The GoPro Hero 13 can manually adjust the white balance value, which is undoubtedly beneficial in these unpredictable lighting conditions.

- **Exposure Control:** This feature allows you to adjust the exposure to ensure that it does not become excessively black or light. This is provided as a highly beneficial alternative in the most adverse illumination conditions.
- **Bitrate:** Produces videos of superior quality; however, it necessitates additional storage. This must be taken into account when documenting extremely detailed scenes.

Creating Custom Presets

1. Turn on the GoPro Hero 13 and navigate to the main menu by swiping down. Select the "**Presets**" option by tapping it.
2. Tap and choose the most suitable preset for the environment in which the shooting is taking place. Assuming that you intend to capture action-packed scenes, the "Activity" preset should be selected as the foundation for this video editing project.

3. **Adjust the Settings:**
    - **Frame rate and resolution:** Modify these to suit your requirements. For example, action images of exceptional quality can be captured at a frame rate of 60 frames per second in 4K.
    - **Field of View:** Verify that the appropriate FOV is being employed. Occasionally, it can be advantageous to employ SuperView for landscapes and Linear for portraits.
    - **Stabilization:** Make certain that HyperSmooth is enabled in a high-movement environment.
    - **White Balance:** Utilize the manual white balance setting consistent with the lighting conditions. 5500K is suitable for clear daylight, while 3200K is appropriate for interior environments.
    - **Exposure:** The exposure parameters can be adjusted to accommodate intense sunlight or shadowy areas.
4. After selecting your preset, save it by selecting the "**Save**" icon and naming it according to the environment, such as "**Outdoor Bright**" or "**Indoor Low Light**."
5. Your configurations are currently preserved and can be accessed without any issues. To navigate between presets, swipe down on the primary screen, select "**Presets**," and then select the appropriate preset for your current environment.

Optimization Presets for Specific Environments

- **Outdoor (sunny settings):**
    - **Resolution and Frame Rate:** 4K at 30 frames per second
    - **Field of View (FOV):** SuperView is used to capture landscapes from a wide angle.
    - HyperSmooth is enabled.
    - **White Balance:** 5500K
    - **Exposure:** -0.5 to prevent overexposure of images in bright conditions
- **Indoors (low-light settings):**
    - **Resolution and Frame Rate:** 1080p at 30 frames per second
    - **FOV:** Linear, to prevent distortion in low-light conditions
    - **HyperSmooth:** Enabled, but with a low intensity
    - **White Balance:** 3200K
    - **Exposure:** +0.5 to enhance the brightness of the scene
- **Action-High Movement Settings:**
    - **Resolution and frame rate:** 2.7k at 120fps for slow motion
    - **FOV:** Wide
    - **HyperSmooth:** On (maximum setting).
    - **White Balance:** Auto (as a result of the swiftly altering conditions)
    - **Exposure:** 0.0 to achieve a balance between highlights and shadows

Testing and Refining

Upon completion of the design of your presets the subsequent phase will involve testing them in actual environments. If the original configurations require refinement, GoPro's touchscreen interface facilitates relatively rapid and effortless settings adjustments. Allocate some time to experiment with various parameters to achieve the best configuration for each environment.

Preset Backup and Sharing

Lastly, it would be prudent to back up your newly edited configurations using the GoPro app. In this manner, you will be able to revert to the original settings when you recalibrate the camera or even share them with other GoPro users if your optimized settings are beneficial to them as well.

Audio Tuning: How to Get the Right Balance Between Sound and Enhanced Voice Clarity

The GoPro Hero 13 offers sophisticated audio customization options, enabling users to tailor their audio capture to their requirements. This feature is especially advantageous for individuals who wish to achieve a harmonious equilibrium between clear vocal capture and natural ambient sound. Consequently, it is suitable for a diverse array of recording environments, including action-packed excursions and vlog-style content.

Balanced Sound Profile

The Hero 13 is equipped with a "**Balanced**" audio profile, which is designed to capture audio that is as accurate as feasible. This configuration is intended to offer a comprehensive aural experience, with the ambiance's sound remaining natural and voices being audible, albeit not excessively so. This profile is best for documenting the environment in a manner that is as authentic as possible, whether it is used to film outdoor activities, concerts, or everyday scenes.

When to Use: When it is necessary to record the complete range of sounds in one's environment, the balanced sound profile is implemented. This is beneficial for travel videos, nature documentaries, and scenarios in which the ambient sound plays a significant role in the narrative.

Enhanced Voice Clarity Mode

The "**Enhanced Voice**" feature of the Hero 13 is particularly useful when voice intelligibility is a critical factor, such as during an interview, vlog, or instructional video. It amplifies vocal frequencies to ensure that the spoken word is audible and distinct. This is accomplished by allowing ambient noises to play in the background at a low volume, rather than filtering them out. Shooting on location in areas with significant background noise, such as wind and other interfering noises, can be beneficial. This applies to both indoor and outdoor locations.

When to Use: Use Enhanced Voice when recording dialogue or narration in an environment with a high level of background noise. It will guarantee that your voice is the focal point of the audio, thereby facilitating the comprehension of the content by the audience.

Automatic Switching and Real-Time Adjustments

The Hero 13 is capable of autonomously transitioning between these audio profiles in response to the detected audio levels and the environment. The audio input is continually analyzed by the embedded software in the camera. Consequently, it is capable of implementing real-time modifications to any of the detected instances. For instance, the Hero 13 can activate Enhanced Voice mode in response to an abrupt increase in background commotion to ensure that vocals remain exceptionally distinct.

Customization: The GoPro app or the camera's variably intuitive touchscreen can also be used to customize audio. This level of customization enables more precise management of the final audio output for each recording session.

Multi-Microphone System

The Audio Tuning settings on the Hero 13 Black, which is equipped with a multi-microphone system, enable users to position multiple microphones around the camera to capture sound from all angles, thereby providing a more immersive audio experience. The camera will be able to utilize only selective microphone input following the selected audio mode to improve vocal intelligibility or balance the overall sound.

Performance: In Balanced mode, the Hero 13 activates the microphones to record the noises of the environment. This results in a sound that is enveloping. Conversely, in Enhanced Voice mode, the system prioritizes the microphones that are situated close to the speaker. This is how the voice is captured with the least amount of interference from the background commotion.

Practical Applications

A significant number of creative capabilities can be unlocked by the sophisticated audio settings on the GoPro Hero 13 Black, which range in complexity from the basic to the extensive. These settings provide the flexibility necessary for the expanding number of content creators who must frequently transition between various types of footage, such as action scenes, and then provide commentary, to produce professional-quality audio without the need to spend an excessive amount of time on post-production work.

- **Vloggers:** Your voice can penetrate the commotion generated by cityscapes or windy conditions with the assistance of the Enhanced Voice mode.
- **Action Sports:** Balanced mode creates a sense of participation in the action while simultaneously eliciting enthusiasm in the environment.

Going Into ProTune: Exposure, White Balance, and ISO Manually

The GoPro Hero 13 is equipped with a sophisticated feature known as ProTune, which provides users with extensive control over their video settings to make professional adjustments. The following is a comprehensive explanation of the manual process for establishing the ISO, white balance, and exposure in ProTune:

Exposure Control

The ProTune Exposure Settings feature enables you to control the amount of light that reaches the camera, a critical factor in achieving the appropriate exposure for the given circumstances.

- Compensation for EV This option will modify the overall luminance of your video. The range is -2.0 to +2.0, with a 0.5 increment. The image is darkened as the value is decreased. An illustration of this is a scene that is excessively illuminated. The image is brightened by increasing the value. A situation in which there is inadequate lighting would serve as an appropriate illustration.

Example: To reduce the brightness and preserve the details in the highlights, you can set your EV Comp to -1.0 when filming in a brightly illuminated outdoor environment.

- **Shutter Speed:** This is the duration of time during which the sensor is permitted to accumulate light. It is possible to manually adjust it using ProTune. For instance, slower shutter velocities, such as 1/60, would permit a greater amount of light to enter, resulting in motion blur that is particularly effective in low-light conditions. For instance, fast shutter velocities (1/120) do not capture any movements, rendering them appropriate for full-action scenes.

Use the following to achieve a cinematic appearance: For example, to achieve 60 frames per second, double your frame rate, such as 1/120.

White Balance

White Balance establishes the color temperature of your footage, ensuring that whites are accurately represented and colors are accurate.

- **Auto White Balance:** The GoPro automatically adjusts the color temperature to match the environment. ProTune enables you to independently establish the color temperature, ensuring that the outcomes are consistent across multiple photos.

ISO Settings

The sensitivity of the camera to light is regulated by the ISO, which influences both the exposure and noise in the footage.

- **ISO Minimum and ISO Maximum:** Protune enables you to establish the minimum and maximum ISOs, which will be automatically adjusted in real-world images based on the brightness of the image. In general, the lower the ISO (e.g., 100), the cleaner the image will be, with less noise, but more light is required. Conversely, the higher the ISO (e.g., 1600), the more sensitive it is to low light and can introduce some noise.

Set the ISO Min to 100 and the ISO Max to 400 in broad daylight conditions. In low-light situations, it can be advantageous to utilize an ISO Min of 400 and an ISO Max of 1600.

- **Locking ISO:** In an environment where the illumination remains constant, it is possible to achieve consistent exposure by setting both the ISO Min and ISO Max to the same value, which is akin to securing the ISO.

For instance, sustaining an ISO of 800 during an indoor photograph will facilitate the achievement of consistent exposure without fluctuations in brightness levels.

Using ProTune for Professional Results

This feature is quite robust on the GoPro Hero 13, enabling you to adjust your settings to achieve the best possible results in any shooting situation. Knowing these manual controls inherently enhances the quality of your footage and provides you with even more creative control, whether you are capturing a fast-paced scene of speedsters or the tranquil beauty of a landscape.

CHAPTER NINE
ADVANCED CINEMATOGRAPHY TECHNIQUES

Filmmaking with the Hero 13: From Action Sequences to Documentaries

The GoPro Hero 13 is a versatile action camera that can be employed in a wide range of cinematic projects, including intimate documentaries and high-octane action sequences. It is not a one-dimensional device.

Here is how you can leverage its sophisticated capabilities to improve your filmmaking:

Mastering the New Modular Lenses

The Hero 13 is the pioneer of a modular series of lenses that enhance the capabilities of your camera in a variety of shooting scenarios:

- **Ultra-Wide Lens Mod:** This 177-degree ultra-wide-angle lens is ideal for capturing dynamic action scenes or expansive landscapes. To enhance the potential for storytelling, attach the device to capture more of the environment in your frame or to create immersive POV views.
- **Macro Lens Mod:** This lens is best for capturing close-ups in high detail, making it an ideal choice for documentaries that require a focus on small objects or minute details. Variable focus enables you to seamlessly transition between close-ups and distant images.
- **Anamorphic Lens Mod:** This lens is an essential component of filmmaking, as it offers a cinematic 21:9 aspect ratio that is both epic and cinematic. It creates dramatic lens flares and minimizes distortion, which are frequently linked to feature films.

Using High-Resolution Capabilities

The Hero 13 allows filmmakers to capture ultra-high-definition footage by supporting 5.3K at 60fps and 4K at 120fps. This resolution is optimal for projects that necessitate highly detailed imagery or for photos that you intend to crop or magnify in post-production without compromising quality.

- **Slow Motion Mastery:** The ability to film at 400 frames per second in 720p allows for the creation of dramatic sequences in which each frame is executed flawlessly. Slow motion is undoubtedly advantageous when filming action sequences, as it enhances the impact and excitement of fast-paced movements in the captured footage.

Professional Level Color Grading with HLG HDR

The Hero 13 is compatible with broadcast standards and supports Hybrid Log Gamma HDR, a format that provides a broader color gamut than traditional HDR. This is crucial for filmmakers who intend to perform extensive color grading in post-production, as it will provide them with greater flexibility and precision in altering the color and exposure.

- **Shooting for Post-Production:** The camera can capture the widest spectrum of colors and detail by maintaining the HLG HDR mode during the shooting process. This enables a greater degree of flexibility in post-processing, enabling the incorporation of creative decisions to produce a visually stunning final product.

Dynamic Shots with Smoother Stabilization

The Hero 13's HyperSmooth 6.0 stabilization, which has been recognized with an Emmy Award, is essential for capturing stable, stable footage in handheld or action images, even in the most hectic environments.

- **360-degree Horizon Lock:** This feature ensures that the horizon line remains consistent regardless of the camera's orientation. This is particularly beneficial in action situations where the camera's orientation can fluctuate swiftly, such as during mountain biking or skiing sequences.

Creative Use of Time-Lapse and Slo-Mo Mode

The Hero 13's TimeWarp and Time Lapse modes are improved by enhancing the resolution and frame rate, as follows:

- **TimeWarp:** This feature enables the creation of dynamic, moving time-lapses in which the camera's position is altered throughout the image. Ideal for illustrating the passage of time in any documentary image, from the bustling activity of a marketplace to the movement of light across a landscape.
- **Slow-Mo:** The new 13x Burst Slo-Mo mode at 720p 400fps captures all the details of fast-moving subjects. It can be particularly effective for emphasizing the most thrilling moments in your footage or for dramatic scene revelations.

Tapping into Audio Personalisation for Documentaries

Audio is equally critical to filmmaking as visuals, and Hero 13 offers a degree of customization in terms of audio settings.

- **True-to-Life Sound Balance:** This would be ideal for documenting natural ambient soundscapes, which is a common practice in documentary work. Utilize this when you desire the audio to accurately represent the actual environment without sacrificing clarity.
- **Voice Enhancement:** This feature will increase the clarity of the vocalists to ensure that the dialogues are as clear as possible, even in a noisy environment, if your production involves interviews or a significant number of voiceovers.

Practical Mounting Solutions

The ball joint mounts provide versatile mounting options that can be swiftly adjusted between photos, and the new Snap and Go Magnetic Latch Mounting system is illustrated below:

- **Magnetic Latch Mounting:** Ideal for rapid adjustments in perspective during filming. For instance, you could transition seamlessly from a chest mount to a helmet mount during action sequences, ensuring that the camera is prepared to capture every moment.

Cinematic Techniques: Using the Anamorphic Lens Mod on Shooting of Movie-Style Footage

The Anamorphic Lens Mod is a revolutionary feature of the GoPro Hero 13 that transforms the appearance and feel of your action camera images to resemble those of a film. This will be extremely beneficial for filmmakers who wish to imbue their footage with a professional appearance.

Advanced cinematography can be achieved by utilizing this instrument in the following manner:

Understanding the Anamorphic Lens Mod

- **Aspect Ratio and Cinematic Feel:** The GoPro Hero 13 is capable of capturing images in the 21:9 aspect ratio, which is the standard format for cinematic widescreen. This is due to the Anamorphic Lens Mod. This provides a broad field of view, which will enhance the cinematic quality of your footage. In addition, it generates subtle lens flares, a characteristic that is frequently observed in high-budget films, which further enhances the cinematic aesthetic and atmosphere.

- **De-squeezing for post-production:** The anamorphic lens alteration compresses the image horizontally. This process is referred to as "squeezing." Subsequently, the camera or editing software "**de-squeezes**" the image, thereby reestablishing the correct widescreen aspect ratio of the image. This can occur during the review process or the editing process. This technique is advantageous in that it captures a greater amount of detail in the scene and retains a significant amount of information from the periphery, resulting in a more dynamic and richer image.

Techniques of Shooting with Anamorphic Lens

- **Framing for Drama:** The framing will differ when using an anamorphic lens. The aspect ratio is wider, which allows for a greater amount of the scene to be in-frame. Therefore, it is recommended to move structures and objects from the perimeter of the frame. This enhances the context and depth of your images, ranging from dynamic action to a cityscape to a landscape.
- **Creating Depth with Foreground Elements:** To optimize the capabilities of an anamorphic lens, incorporate foreground elements into your composition whenever feasible. In addition to improving the scene's profundity, it also enhances the viewer's immersion in the action. For example, the cinematic experience is significantly improved by the parallax effect that is generated when a subject is recorded as it moves through space, with foreground elements such as trees and buildings in the frame.

Maximize Features on GoPro Hero 13

- **HyperSmooth 6.0:** The Anamorphic Lens Mod is seamlessly integrated with the in-camera HyperSmooth stabilization of the Hero 13, ensuring that even handheld or motion photos are

both stable and smooth. It maintains its stabilization to ensure that the footage remains cinematic and captures the scene precisely during fast-action images.
- **In-camera setting changes:** The default camera settings would have been modified automatically upon the attachment of the Anamorphic Lens Mod to the GoPro Hero 13. This would encompass the most suitable frame rates and resolutions for the intended cinematic effect. Experiment with frame rates to further refine these, such as capturing high-detail slow-motion images at 60fps or using traditional film at 24fps.

Post-Production Tips

- **Color grading for a cinematic look:** After the footage has been captured, color grading will help elevate it to a cinematic quality. The majority of anamorphic footage is visually appealing, with mellow tones and subtle contrast adjustments that emphasize its filmic quality. Color grading tools can be implemented in your editing software by modifying the shadows, mid-tones, and highlights to achieve your desired aesthetic style.
- **Cinematic Bars Addition:** Even though this Anamorphic Lens Mod captures the footage in a wide-screen format, you can still wish to incorporate black bars at the top and bottom of the frame in the post-production process to enhance the cinematic experience. If you have a combination of anamorphic footage and other lens camera views, it is also simple to standardize the appearance.

Practical Applications

- **Short Films and Documentaries:** The anamorphic lens conversion is an excellent choice for indie filmmakers and documentarians who wish to enhance the cinematic quality of their footage without the need to invest in typically more expensive camera systems. Even the most mundane scene is rendered epic and captivating by the wide field of view and a unique set of visual characteristics.
- **Action Sequences:** The Anamorphic Lens Mod with sophisticated stabilization in GoPro Hero 13 ensures that your footage remains sharp, stable, and cinematic, whether it is a high-speed car pursuit, an extreme sports sequence, or a dramatic scene with characters moving quickly.

How to Use Slow-Motion Creatively in Storytelling

The filmmaker employs catalysis, particularly in slow motion, to attest to the emotional profundity and emphasis of certain scenes in his film. Presently, the GoPro Hero 13 offers novel opportunities for inventive slow-motion storytelling, with a maximum frame rate of 400 frames per second at 720p and 120 frames per second at 4K.

These capabilities can be leveraged to enhance your cinematic endeavors in the following manner:

Highlighting Significant Events

- **Method:** The most significant aspects of your narrative should be emphasized through the use of slow motion. Slow-motion footage enables your audience to appreciate the intricacy of a variety

of events, including the collision of a wave with a surfboard, the expression of joy on a person's face, or the exploding of confetti during a celebration.
- **Performance:** Record those moments at the maximum frame rate possible, such as 400 fps at 720p. The post will slow down, enabling the viewer to experience the full impact of the event, which is both visually spectacular and emotionally resonant.

Create Suspense and Tension
- **Technique:** Employ slow motion to create a sense of suspense, and then allow the audience to speculate on the next event. This could occur in action sequences or any other location that is subject to unpredictability.
- **Execution:** Capture highly detailed, high-resolution screenshots with the GoPro Hero 13 at 120fps in 4K. For instance, an actor who is advancing toward a portal or an athlete who is in mid-air at the apex of a leap should be slowed down. The action pauses, and the viewer holds their breath with bated breath.

Improving Emotional Impact
- **Technique:** Slow motion is frequently necessary to bolster emotionally charged moments. Slowing down the action enables an audience to engage more deeply with the emotions being depicted, whether they are pleasure, anguish, triumph, or defeat.
- **Execution:** As a compromise between resolution and frame rate, record at 240 frames per second in 2.7K. The scenes in which the character is overcome with emotion, such as a hearty embrace or a falling tear down the cheek, are rendered poignantly profound and affecting by slowing down the footage.

Details with Macro Shots
- **Technique:** The Macro Lens Mod on the GoPro Hero 13 enables the capture of minute details, a moment before they zoom past. The intricacy of nature or the complete beauty of commonplace objects would be even more startling to the observers in slow motion.
- **Execution:** Utilize the Macro Lens Mod and capture images at either 120 fps or 240 fps, contingent upon your resolution requirements. Use slow motion to add an artistic flourish to your storytelling, such as a drop of water descending onto a surface or the flutter of an insect's wings.

Shooting Epic Action Shots
- **Technique:** Slow motion is a highly effective method for demonstrating high-intensity actions or action sports, allowing the viewer to appreciate each movement with greater precision and skill.
- **Performance:** Record high-resolution action sequences at 5.3K 60fps or opt for ultra-slow motion at 720p 400fps. From a surfer carving reverse on a wave to a mountain biker carving singletrack, each of these can be reduced to a fraction-of-a-second slo-mo to emphasize the force of the movement and the expertise of the athlete.

Enhancing the Cinematic Feel with Anamorphic Lenses
- **Technique:** The GoPro Hero 13 Anamorphic Lens Mod, which is scheduled for release in 2025, will enable you to capture cinematic, wide-angle views with less distortion and dramatic lens effects. This, in conjunction with slow motion, will professionally render your footage, reminiscent of a cinematic film.
- **Performance:** Utilize an Anamorphic Lens Mod to record in 21:9 format at 120fps or 240fps. Enhance the theatrical and visual allure of scenes by employing slow motion, particularly those that involve high-speed action or dramatic illumination changes. The combination of slow motion and widescreen format can result in nearly majestic footage.

Telling a Story Through Visual Contrast
- **Technique:** To illustrate the distinction between calm and sudden action, or to contrast one scene with another, contrast slow motion and real-time.
- **Shooting:** Utilize varying frame rates to film in front of contrasting scenes. Perhaps a real-time video of a serene, tranquil landscape could be captured, followed by a slow-motion action scene to disrupt the tranquility. This can be quite effective in terms of visual and affective contrast, which helps to maintain the narrative's momentum.

Using Sound Design in Slow-Motion
- **Technique:** Slow motion, while providing a visual effect, can also have an impact on the aural component.
- **Action:** Attempt to re-edit the video and audio to achieve a dreamlike effect by slowing down the audio in conjunction with the video, or contrast it with a fast-paced soundtrack to increase the drama. The GoPro Hero 13 offers a more sophisticated method of customizing audio, allowing you to maintain the clarity of voices or preserve ambient noises, allowing for even more inventive sound design options in your film.

Key Takeaways
- Employ slow motion to emphasize individual moments, heighten the emotional impact, and create a sense of anticipation.
- Macro images and anamorphic lenses for a more cinematic effect—details
- The visuals could be enhanced by a combination of real-time and slow motion, and the aural design could be utilized to emphasize the contrast.

Working with Other Gear: Drones, Gimbals, and External Microphones

The GoPro Hero 13 is a potent instrument for capturing high-quality footage, particularly when it is paired with other equipment, such as external microphones, gimbals, and drones.

Drones: Aerial Cinematography

You can capture magnificent aerial views that add a new dimension to your videos by mounting your GoPro Hero 13 on a drone. To optimize this configuration, follow these steps:

- **Mounting:** The drone should be capable of mounting a GoPro Hero 13. The majority of drones from influential brands, such as DJI, are equipped with pre-set mounts or gimbals that ensure the stability of cameras, even at challenging angles. Utilize the Snap and Go Magnetic Latch Mounting system on the GoPro to ensure a secure attachment during custom rigging.
- **Optimize the Settings:** The Hero 13's default 5.3K 60fps setting enables the capture of high-resolution aerial footage. Enable HyperSmooth stabilization to achieve seamless aerial photos, which is crucial for reducing the drone's vibrational sensation during movement.
- **Lens Mods:** The Ultra-Wide Lens Mod is the best choice for aerial shooting, as it provides a 177-degree field of view, allowing for the capture of a wider range of landscapes. The Horizon Leveling feature ensures that your footage remains consistent, regardless of the drone's inclination.
- **Battery Management:** The length of the flight can be a concern because the batteries are depleted by the attachments required to mount the GoPro onto a drone. Nevertheless, the Hero 13's 1,900mAh battery provides a maximum of 1.5 hours of recording time at high resolutions. Increasing the duration of a session can be achieved by utilizing reserve batteries or external power sources, such as those provided by a specific drone.

Gimbals: Stabilized Ground Footage

Smooth, professional footage necessitates the use of gimbals on the ground. The GoPro Hero 13 boasts advanced stabilization capabilities that, when combined with a gimbal, can produce remarkably stable images.

- **Gimbal Compatibility:** It is important to ensure that your gimbal is compatible with the Hero 13 Black, as the camera weighs 159g. Most gimbals, including the DJI Osmo and FeiyuTech G6, have been equipped with mounts that accommodate GoPros. The transition between handheld photography and a gimbal setup is also made relatively simple by the magnetic mounting mechanism on the Hero 13.
- **Calibration and Balance:** Ensure that the gimbal is properly balanced with the GoPro affixed to it to prevent unnecessary drifting. To prevent stressing the motors, additional accessories affixed on the GoPro, such as lens mods or external microphones, must be correctly balanced on the gimbal.
- **Shooting Modes:** Utilize the gimbal's stabilization capabilities in conjunction with the Hero 13's high-frame-rate modes, such as 120fps at 4K. It will be ideal for capturing dynamic movements such as cycling, jogging, or sports.
- **Low-Light Enhancements:** The Hero 13's enhanced low-light capabilities, when combined with a gimbal, will result in clear and seamless footage, even in low-light conditions. TimeWarp and Night Lapse modes enable the creation of creatively stabilized time-lapse sequences.

External Microphones: Improved Audio Quality

The audio quality of the GoPro Hero 13 will be considerably improved, particularly in challenging environments, when an external microphone is used, even though the internal microphones are now more advanced and the audio quality can be adjusted.

- **Microphone Selection:** Select an external microphone that is compatible with the GoPro's USB-C port, such as the Rode VideoMicro or GoPro Media Mod.
- **Mounting:** The GoPro Media Mod is an excellent accessory for external microphones, as it not only provides a 3.5mm mic interface but also enables the microphone to be readily mounted atop the camera for vlogging or interviewing.
- **Settings:** GoPro offers audio parameters that are contingent upon the location of the action. Hero 13 does provide the capability to select from a variety of pre-set audio profiles. Try the Voice setting: this mode prioritizes vocal clarity without forsaking ambient sounds, a critical feature when recording outdoors in noisy conditions.
- **Wind Reduction:** Utilize a windshield or the built-in wind noise reduction feature of your Hero 13 camera when shooting in gusty conditions. Furthermore, the inclusion of an external microphone with a deceased cat on it provides an additional layer of protection against atmospheric noise.

Final Tips

- **Audio Syncing:** If you are employing an external recorder, applaud at the commencement of the recording to facilitate audio synchronization during post-production.
- **Firmware update:** It is recommended that you update the firmware of your GoPro Hero 13 periodically to ensure compatibility with the most recent equipment and to take advantage of any newly added features.

CHAPTER TEN
MOUNTING YOUR GOPRO HERO 13

Overview of GoPro mounts and accessories

GoPro Hero 13 features a variety of sophisticated mounting systems that enhance the safety, simplicity of use, and flexibility of the device while it is being used to capture an adventure.

Magnetic Latch Mounting System

The new Magnetic Latch Mounting system, which is a feature of the Hero 13 Black, is intended to simplify the process of installing and removing the camera. Users will be able to mount the camera more rapidly with this system than with traditional bolt mounting. It is constructed from robust magnets that ensure the camera remains securely in position and enable users to effortlessly attach and detach it from a variety of attachments.

Benefits:

- **Convenience and Speed:** The magnetic fastener simplifies the process of mounting for individuals who frequently need to replace their mounts.
- **Versatility:** Capable of operating on any metal mounting surface and in a variety of positions to produce innovative angles and images.
- **Safety:** The magnets were sufficiently robust to prevent the camera from detaching during high-speed activities, despite their ease of use.

This system is especially beneficial during action scenes, where every minute is crucial and the user must either reposition or remove the camera without the need for fasteners.

Built-In Mounting Fingers

The Hero 13 is equipped with GoPro's integrated mounting digits. This action camera can be mounted on a variety of GoPro mounts without the need for additional housing or adaptors, as a result of the foldable digits located at the bottom of the camera.

Benefits:

- **Low-Profile Mounting:** The mounting fingers will establish a secure and low-profile connection, thereby reducing camera movement and vibration by holding the camera closer to the mounting surface.
- **Compatibility:** These fingers are interoperable with all GoPro mounts that utilize the traditional GoPro attachment system, simplifying the process of integrating with existing accessories and configurations.
- **Durability:** The digits are engineered to withstand extreme activities, including impact, grime, and water, to maintain the camera's position.

GoPro's trademark is the mounting fingers, which strike a balance between reliability and convenience.

1/4-20 Mounting Threads

The Hero 13 is equipped with 1/4-20 mounting fittings, in addition to the magnetic clasp and mounting fingers. These are the standard fittings that are used in the majority of professional cameras to mount a GoPro on tripods, rigs, or other camera accessories that are not specifically intended for GoPro cameras.
Benefits:

- **Professional Flexibility:** The 1/4-20 fittings provide a wide range of mounting options, particularly for professional videographers and photographers who may wish to incorporate GoPro into their existing infrastructure.
- **Wider Accessory Compatibility:** The inclusion of such connections will enable the Hero 13 to be compatible with a broader selection of accessories, including those that were not originally designed for GoPro cameras.

- **Stable Mounting:** When the camera is used with professional tripods and mounts, these fittings are extremely stable and secure in attachment. This is crucial for capturing high-quality footage.

GoPro's versatility is generally enhanced by these threads, which render the camera more appealing to a diverse array of users, including professional filmmakers and casual adventurers.

Underwater and adventure use: Preparing your GoPro for extreme conditions

Careful preparation is necessary to guarantee that the GoPro Hero 13 functions optimally and remains safeguarded when utilized for underwater filming and other extreme adventure activities. Here are a few suggestions and recommended accessories to optimize your GoPro's performance in these circumstances:

1. **Waterproofing and Housing Options**

Without the need for any additional shielding, the GoPro Hero 13 is inherently weatherproof up to 33 feet (10 meters). Nevertheless, if you intend to delve deeper, it is imperative to acquire additional impermeable housing:

- **Diving Housing:** An impermeable housing that is rated for a minimum of 196 feet (60 meters) is required for scuba diving or unrestricted diving below 33 feet. This will guarantee that the camera is safeguarded from water and pressure harm at greater depths.
- **Lens Protection:** Camera lenses can be subjected to severe conditions in underwater environments. It is advisable to employ a protective lens cover or dive-specific lens accessory that are resistant to saline corrosion and dents.
2. **Utilize anti-fog inserts.**

The camera's lens can become foggy when working in frigid water or transitioning between warm and cool environments. To prevent this:

- **Anti-Fog Inserts:** Insert anti-fog inserts into the impermeable housing. These absorb moisture and minimize condensation, thereby guaranteeing crystal-clear footage.
- **Dry the Camera:** Before securing the camera in the enclosure, ensure that the camera is entirely dry. Additionally, it is possible to prevent condensation by storing the camera and enclosure in a dry environment before embarking on your adventure.

3. **Preparing for Low-Light Conditions**

Even during the day, underwater lighting is frequently less intense than that on land:

- Set the ISO and shutter speed to a higher value (e.g., 800-1600) and a delayed shutter speed to allow for a greater amount of light to reach the sensor. Nevertheless, it is important to exercise caution when adjusting the ISO setting, as the introduction of noise can occur at higher values.
- **Use External Lights:** To illuminate the environment, it is advisable to employ impermeable lamps that are compatible with GoPro. These lamps assist in enhancing the visibility of colors and details that can appear washed out or faint in the natural underwater light.

4. **White Balance and Color Correction**

Water's ability to refract light can influence the colors that are documented in your footage:

- **Manual White Balance:** Adjust the white balance manually to better accommodate underwater conditions. Switch to a custom white balance for deeper water or specific illumination conditions, while using "Auto" for shallow water.
- **Color filters:** Opt for red filters for blue water (e.g., oceans) or magenta filters for green water (e.g., lakes). These filters assist in compensating for the absence of red light in underwater footage, thereby enhancing its natural appearance.

5. **Stabilization and Mounting for Adventure Use**

Stabilization and mounting are indispensable for hazardous sports such as surfing, mountain bicycling, or skiing:

- **HyperSmooth Stabilization:** The Hero 13's HyperSmooth stabilization guarantees consistent footage during high-intensity activities. To reduce shakiness in action shots, activate this feature.
- **Adventure-Specific Mounts:**
    - **Helmet or Chest Mount:** These devices offer a first-person perspective, which enhances the immersive quality of the footage.
    - **Handlebar or Surfboard Mount:** These devices are ideal for bicycling, surfing, or other similar activities, as they ensure the camera remains stable on the equipment.
- **Quick-Release Mounts:** Consider the use of quick-release mounts for activities that can require the rapid exchange of mounts or the detachment of the camera, as they provide greater flexibility.

6. **Battery Life Management**

Battery efficacy can be significantly impacted by extreme conditions, particularly in frigid environments:

- **Use Enduro Battery:** The Hero 13's Enduro battery provides enhanced performance in frigid temperatures and extended shooting periods. Ensure that you have extra batteries on hand to replace them during extended adventures.
- **Keep Batteries Warm:** To ensure that spare batteries remain charged in frigid weather, keep them in an insulated pocket that is near your body.

7. **Protective Covers and Cases**

Rough handling and exposure to grime, dust, or impacts are frequently associated with adventure use.

- **Protective Casing:** To prevent the camera from scratches and impacts, it is recommended to use silicone or polymer protective coverings.
- **Lens Cover or Cap:** Protect the lens with a cover when it is not in use to prevent damage, particularly when navigating rugged environments.

8. **Post-Adventure Care**

It is essential to conduct proper maintenance after an adventure to ensure the longevity of your camera:

- Rinse the camera thoroughly with fresh water to remove salt, grit, and detritus if it is used in saline or dusty environments. This serves as an inhibitor of corrosion and injury.
- Camera Drying and Inspection: Ensure that the camera is thoroughly dried, with a particular emphasis on the battery compartment and seals, and that it is inspected for any obvious evidence of damage.

Using GoPro Mods (Media Mod, Light Mod, Display Mod) to expand functionality

The GoPro Hero 13's Mods—Media Mod, Light Mod, and Display Mod—enable users to enhance the camera's functionality, thereby increasing its adaptability to a variety of shooting scenarios. The capabilities of the GoPro are improved by each mod, and their appropriate use is delineated below:

Media Mod

The Media Mod is a frame-style accessory that enhances the GoPro Hero 13's capabilities as a video production tool by providing additional connections and mounting options.

- **Built-in Directional Microphone:**
    - The Media Mod is equipped with a directional microphone that enhances the audio quality of the camera's standard microphones. It is intended to ensure that voice capture is prioritized while ambient noise is minimized, rendering it suitable for vlogging, interviews, or any scenario in which clear audio is crucial.
    - **External Microphone Input (3.5mm Jack):** The Media Mod provides a 3.5mm input for the attachment of an external microphone, such as a Lavalier or shotgun mic, if you require even higher audio fidelity or have specific audio requirements.
- **Extra Ports and Connectivity:**

- o **HDMI Output:** The Media Mod is equipped with a Micro HDMI interface, which enables the GoPro to be connected to an external monitor or TV for real-time playback or live broadcasting.
  - o **USB-C Port:** The Media Mod offers an additional USB-C port for data transmission and charging, even when other accessories are affixed, in addition to the camera's existing USB-C port.
- **Cold Shoe Mounts:**
  - o The Media Mod is equipped with two cold shoe attachments that can be used to affix accessories, such as the Light Mod, an external microphone, or other equipment, such as a small monitor. This enhances the adaptability of your camera configuration, rendering it suitable for more intricate filming scenarios.

Best Use Cases:

- Setups for vlogging or streaming that require superior audio quality.
- Situations in which it is necessary to mount multiple accessories.
- Utilizing external monitors or recording devices through HDMI output.

Light Mod

The Light Mod is a compact LED light accessory that can be used independently or attached to the GoPro. It is sufficiently potent to satisfy a variety of illumination requirements, including as a fill light in brilliant environments or low light.

- **High levels of brightness:**
  - o The Light Mod offers a luminosity of up to 200 lumens, which can be adjusted to four different levels: low, medium, high, and strobe. This renders it appropriate for a variety of situations, including nocturnal outdoor environments and dimly illuminated indoor spaces.
  - o Impervious Design: The Light Mod is impervious to a depth of 33 feet (10 meters), allowing you to use it in damp conditions without concern. It is best for underwater cinematography or shooting in rainy environments.
- **Compatibility with Media Mod:**
  - o It is effortlessly attached to the cold shoe mount of the Media Mod, serving as an integrated illumination solution for video shots.
  - o **Standalone Use:** The Light Mod is also capable of being detached and used independently, rendering it adaptable for off-camera illumination requirements.

Best Use Cases:

- Filming in dim light or at night to illuminate subjects.
- Photographing underwater, where natural light is restricted.
- Action photos necessitate additional illumination to optimize exposure.

Display Mod

The Display Mod enhances the GoPro Hero 13 by incorporating a secondary screen that is oriented forward. This feature is particularly useful for vlogging or self-filming.

- **Flip-Up Screen Design:**

    - When affixed to the Media Mod, the Display Mod features a 2-inch flip-up screen that faces forward. This enables you to observe yourself while recording, thereby guaranteeing that the image is properly framed.
    - **Integrated Battery:** It is equipped with a battery, which prevents the GoPro from depleting its power while in use. The Display Mod is recharged using USB-C.
- **Convenience for Self-Recording:**
    - The mod is particularly beneficial for vloggers, content creators, or individuals who are documenting themselves, as it enables the precise framing and monitoring of the captured content.

Best Use Cases:

- Self-recorded content, such as vlogging.
- Circumstances in which accurately framing the subject is essential.
- The use of a second screen ensures that various perspectives are correctly framed when filming from multiple angles.

Tips for Using GoPro Mods Together

- **Integrating the Media Mod, Light Mod, and Display Mod:**
    - When combined, these modifications establish a potent vlogging or action setup. The Media Mod enhances audio and connectivity, the Light Mod enhances illumination, and the Display Mod guarantees precise framing.
    - **Versatile Mounting:** The Media Mod's cold shoe mounts facilitate the simultaneous attachment of the Light Mod and other accessories, enabling a versatile configuration.
- **Power Management:**
    - When employing multiple modifications, it is important to monitor battery levels, as the addition of accessories can result in faster battery depletion. It is advisable to bring extra batteries or utilize an external power source for extended shoots.

Best Mounts for Different Activities: Cycling, Surfing, Hiking, etc.

The GoPro Hero 13 is equipped with a comprehensive array of mounting options and accessories that have been designed to enhance its adaptability to a wide range of activities.

Cycling

- **Handlebar/Seatpost/Pole Mount:** This mount is perfect for motorcyclists who wish to capture smooth images from the bike's perspective. It is designed to affix securely to either the handlebars

or seat posts, ensuring that your GoPro remains fixed even on bumpy trails. A complete 360-degree rotation is available to facilitate the adjustment of camera angles.
- **Chest Mount:** The chest mount captures the handlebars, your limbs, and the trail ahead, providing a slightly lower but more immersive angle. This could be extremely engaging in mountain bicycling, as it allows the rider to participate in a virtual excursion.
- **Helmet Mount:** The helmet mount is best for obtaining a rider's perspective. It attaches to the top or side of your helmet, providing a soaring vantage point that can capture your line of sight and observe the path ahead. This feature is particularly well-suited for descent mountain biking or road cycling.

Surfing
- **Surfboard Mount:** The GoPro Surfboard Mount is specifically composed for sailors. It is securely fastened to capture images of the waves and your actions from the perspective of the board's deck. The camera will not be severed even if harsh conditions occur due to the tether of the mount, which guarantees additional safety.
- **Bite Mount:** Surfers can capture footage without using their hands with the Bite Mount. To ensure that the surf session is captured undistorted, you hold this implement in your mouth. This apparatus is one of the most highly sought-after devices for recording a point-of-view, as it creates the illusion that the viewer is in the barrel of the wave.
- **Floaty Case:** The Floaty Case is a crucial surfing accessory that will ensure that your GoPro remains afloat if it becomes detached from its mount. Additionally, the camera's visibility in water is enhanced by the vibrant orange case.

Hiking
- **Head Strap + QuickClip:** The Head Strap mount is the perfect choice for trekkers who wish to document their voyage from a perspective angle. It can be adjusted to suit over helmets or directly on your head, which offers a stable and comfortable method of recording the trek.
- **3-Way Grip:** This mount can be utilized as a tripod, an extension arm, or a camera grip to capture a diverse array of images and angles during your trek. The extension arm is designed for wide-angle selfies or group pictures, while the handle provides stability while strolling.
- **Backpack Strap Mount:** The Backpack Strap Mount is a convenient option for trekkers who prefer a hands-free experience. The GoPro is positioned at chest height to capture your trek from over the shoulder by attaching the mount to the strap of your rucksack.

Snowboarding and skiing
- **Ski Pole Mount:** This mount is designed to be attached to your ski pole, allowing you to capture distinctive angles while skiing or snowboarding. It is especially advantageous to capture your maneuvers and stunts from a lower perspective, as the resulting footage will be highly dynamic and action-packed.
- **Helmet Front + Side Mount:** This mount is designed to be attached to the front or side of your helmet and provides a variety of intriguing perspectives. The front mount provides forward-facing

photos, while the side mount provides a wide-angle view of the surrounding environment, which is ideal for those scenic downhill runs.

- **Wrist Strap:** This strap is the best choice for skiers or snowboarders who desire to capture a shot as quickly as feasible. It enables the user to rotate it 360 degrees, thereby capturing footage from the majority of angles without the need to pause. Additionally, it can be adjusted up and down.

Diving

- **Dive Housing:** This dive housing is an essential component of any underwater adventure. It is intended to safeguard the GoPro Hero 13 from mild water, with a maximum depth of 196 feet or 60 meters. In various water conditions, the enclosure improves camera exposure functionality by incorporating filtration.
- **Hand/Arm/Leg/Chest Strap:** This strap mount can be affixed to the hand, arm, leg, or torso, depending on the user's preference. It is the best choice for underwater exploration, as it securely fastens the GoPro and frees your wrists for filmmaking.
- **Dome Port:** A specialized accessory that enables the capturing of split-level images of both the water surface and the air above it simultaneously. This is accomplished by submerging oneself in crystal-clear water and capturing marine life in its natural, organic habitat.

Power and Mounting Accessories: Volta grip, Ball Joint Mount

GoPro Hero 13 surpasses expectations by providing new power and mounting accessories that enhance the user experience in capturing high-quality photos in a variety of environments.

Volta Power Grip

The Volta Power Grip is a versatile accessory that integrates the grip, battery, and remote control into a single unit. The battery life of the GoPro Hero 13 is more than doubled by this accessory, which allows for recording at 5.3K for up to four hours. The Volta is an ideal tool for any vlogger or action enthusiast who requires a camera that can record for an extended period without the need for continual battery replacements. This is due to the camera's built-in controls, which allow for remote operation.

- **Integrated Battery:** The internal battery on the Volta extends the endurance of the GoPro Hero 13 by providing up to three times the number of batteries. It would be beneficial to include a portion of the footage that is longer in duration, such as during travel or extreme sports.
- **Remote Control:** The stabilizer includes a built-in remote control that enables you to effortlessly operate your camera from a distance. This provides added convenience when photographing alone or when your camera is out of reach due to its mount.
- **Compatibility:** The Volta is a versatile addition to the GoPro setup process, as it is compatible with all recent GoPro models and was specifically designed for the Hero 13 Black.

Ball Joint Mount

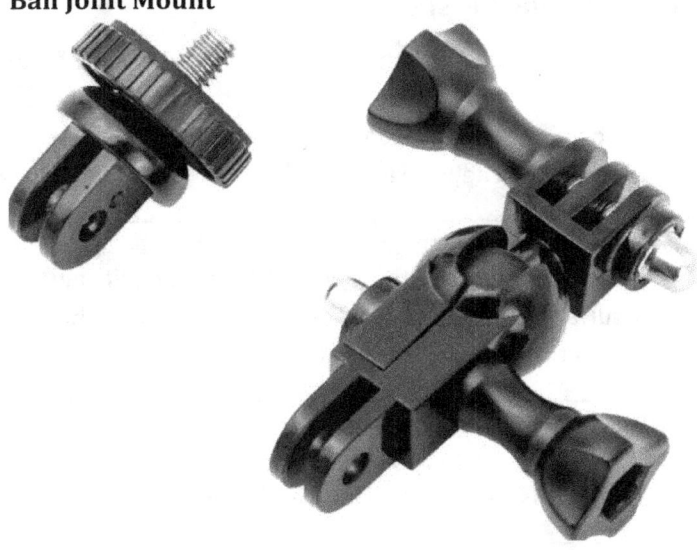

The Ball Joint Mount is the other accessory that offers some practicality in terms of simplicity of operation and flexibility. This mount enables you to revolve your camera 360 degrees to capture images from any perspective without the need to reposition the entire mount.

- **360-Degree Rotation:** The Ball Joint Mount enables the effortless capture of dynamic angles and perspectives with minimal adjustments, allowing for full rotation. This feature is particularly beneficial when capturing action photos, as it allows for the occasional adjustment of the camera's position.
- **Quick-Release Mechanism:** The mounting system employs a quick-release dual-latch mechanism to facilitate the effortless attachment and detachment of the GoPro. It enhances efficacy in situations where it is necessary to frequently transition between different mounting positions.
- **Magnetic Latch Compatibility:** The Ball Joint Mount is compatible with the new Snap and Go Magnetic Latch Mounting system of the Hero 13 Black, enabling the ease of changing mounts or adjusting the camera's orientation.

Other Mount Accessories

The GoPro Hero 13 is compatible with a variety of mounting solutions, in addition to the Volta Power Grip and Ball Joint Mount:

- **Magnetic Latch Mount:** A novel magnetic mounting system that replaces the traditional bolt mount, enabling the camera to be attached to a variety of surfaces more quickly and securely.
- **Built-in Mounting Fingers:** Offer a secure and low-profile mounting option that is compatible with all GoPro accessories.

DIY Mounting Hacks and Ideas to Capture Unique Perspectives

In addition to its improved performance and state-of-the-art features, the GoPro Hero 13 offers an infinite number of capture opportunities due to its adaptable mounting options. Learn how to effectively utilize mounting options while shooting on a GoPro in this comprehensive guide. Additionally, explore some DIY techniques that will elevate your GoPro filming experience to new heights.

Snap and Go Magnetic Latch Mounting System

An innovative magnetic clasp mounting system is integrated into the Hero 13 Black, simplifying the process of mounting the camera to a variety of surfaces. This feature is ideal for individuals who are constantly on the move, as it allows for the rapid and effortless transition between vehicles.

DIY Hack: Magnetic Mount on Metal Surfaces

For a stable platform that enables you to capture distinctive low-angle or high-speed photos, affix a robust neodymium magnet to flat metal surfaces such as car roofs, cycle frames, or metal railings.

Ball Joint Mounts

The Hero 13 is equipped with a ball joint mount that enables the camera to be positioned more easily, as it supports 360-degree rotation. It is an ideal solution for obtaining those challenging angles without the need to modify the entire mount.

DIY Hack: Custom Swivel Mount

Glue a small ball head mount, which is a feature of certain tripods, to a clamp or suction cup base. The homemade swivel mount can be applied to flat surfaces, such as the dashboard or car windows, to facilitate effortless rotation with exceptionally smooth movement. This feature is particularly useful in action sequences such as off-road bicycling or car pursuits, as it produces exceptional dynamic shots.

Built-in Mounting Fingers and 1/4-20 Mounting Threads

The GoPro Hero 13 is equipped with the same traditional built-in mounting fingers, which are compatible with a vast array of GoPro mounts and accessories. Additionally, the 1/4-20 mounting threads facilitate compatibility with conventional tripod attachments.

DIY Hack: Helmet Mounting

Use the built-in mounting fingers to secure the camera to your helmet and capture first-person POV images. Attach the camera with heavy-duty velcro strips if you are feeling particularly DIY. This provides a mounting solution that is both secure and simple to adjust. Ideal for skydiving, snowboarding, or mountain bicycling.

HB-Series Lens Mods

The new series of HB Lens Mods provided you with increased creative control over your footage, including Ultra Wide, Macro, and Anamorphic lenses. The purpose of these lenses was to enhance the camera's capabilities in specific situations.

DIY Hack: Handheld Rig with Lens Mods
Construct a transportable device using a small stabilizer or a modified selfie stick. Use the device to capture stabilized, cinematic images, primarily with an Anamorphic lens to simulate the widescreen effect of a movie. Attach your GoPro to the lens mod of your choice. This is highly beneficial for capturing fluid action photos while on the move, travel documentaries, or vlogging.

Suction Cup and Clamp Mounts
Suction-cup mounts are ideal for securing your GoPro to flat surfaces, such as vehicle hoods or windows, while clamp mounts are effective on irregular surfaces, such as tree branches or handlebars.

DIY Hack: Custom Suction Mount
To ensure that a standard suction cup mount remains in position for underwater or high-speed applications, apply an impermeable adhesive. This is beneficial for recording angles during auto racing, watercraft, or surfing. This can also be attached to a flexible limb, which allows for angle adjustment without the need to modify the mount.

Harness mounts allow you to directly affix the GoPro to your torso or back, capturing an immersive POV shot that depicts the action from your perspective.

DIY Hack: Custom Shoulder Mount

Convert an outdated knapsack strap into a shoulder mount by affixing the GoPro to it with a small mount or fastener. This offers stable and comfortable over-the-shoulder views for activities such as rock climbing, trekking, or any other situation in which it is desirable to maintain both hands-free during filming.

Additional Tips

- **DIY Extension Pole:** Construct an extension pole by utilizing a telescopic rod, similar to one found on a painter's pole. Utilize it for an aerial or follow-up photograph. Ideal for dynamic moving images, landscape views, and group selfies.
- **Underwater Hacks:** To prevent fogging issues in underwater housing, anti-fog inserts or DIY variants that incorporate silica gel sachets into the housing can be implemented. This will guarantee the capture of clear footage during snorkeling or diving.

CONCLUSION

The GoPro Hero 13 is an exceptionally capable camera that can effectively manage virtually any challenge. It equips you with the necessary tools to capture exceptional videos and photographs, whether you are documenting action sports, underwater excursions, or everyday moments. It is engineered to assist you in the production of exceptional content, featuring 5.3K resolution, various frame rates for seamless or slow-motion footage, and built-in image stabilization.

This guide has addressed the fundamentals of camera setup, including the selection of appropriate parameters, the utilization of accessories such as Mods, and the making of adjustments to suit various circumstances. The objective is to instill a sense of assurance in you when operating the Hero 13, regardless of whether you are a novice or have prior experience with GoPro cameras.

Remember that practice makes ideal as you continue to utilize your GoPro. Experiment with various settings and angles, and don't hesitate to be inventive. The more you utilize the camera, the more you will comprehend the settings that are most advantageous for you.

With the knowledge of how to optimize the Hero 13, you are prepared to document your adventures, regardless of their scale, and disseminate them to the world. Take pleasure in your filming and ensure that each image is significant.

INDEX

1

1/4-20 Mounting, **102**
10-bit color, **70**, **71**
10-bit Color, **70**, **71**
10-bit Color Photos, **70**, **71**

3

3-Way Grip, **99**

A

Accessories, **5**, **11**, **12**, **100**, **101**
Action Shots, **72**, **89**
Anamorphic, **50**, **52**, **53**, **54**, **55**, **56**, **85**, **87**, **88**, **90**, **102**, **103**
Audio, **4**, **5**, **10**, **76**, **81**, **82**, **86**, **91**, **92**

B

Backpack Strap Mount, **99**
Ball Joint Mount, **100**, **101**
Ball Joint Mounts, **102**
battery, **viii**, **1**, **3**, **7**, **11**, **12**, **17**, **19**, **20**, **21**, **22**, **28**, **39**, **40**, **41**, **43**, **46**, **47**, **76**, **91**, **96**, **98**, **100**
Battery, **1**, **6**, **11**, **12**, **17**, **20**, **21**, **40**, **41**, **47**, **76**, **91**, **95**, **96**, **98**, **100**
Bite Mount, **99**
Bluetooth, **5**, **26**, **27**, **28**
Burst, **1**, **8**, **20**, **66**, **67**, **68**, **86**
Burst-Shooting, **8**
Button, **12**, **15**, **21**, **22**, **30**
Buttons, **12**

C

Calibration, **91**
Camera, **1**, **11**, **12**, **13**, **21**, **29**, **31**, **35**, **37**, **45**, **69**, **70**, **76**, **94**, **95**, **96**
Chest, **95**, **99**, **100**
Cloud, **30**, **31**, **33**, **35**, **36**
Cloud Backup, **35**
Color Correction, **34**, **95**
Color filters, **95**
Components, **12**
Counter, **20**

Custom Presets, **79**
Custom Streaming, **76**
Cycling, **98**

D

De-squeezing, **87**
dimensions, **38**
Direct Sharing, **33**, **35**
Display, **13**, **18**, **21**, **22**, **96**, **98**
Dive Housing, **100**
Diving, **94**, **100**
Diving Housing, **94**
DIY, **59**, **102**, **103**, **104**
Dome Port, **100**
Drones, **90**

E

Export Options, **35**
Exposure, **45**, **73**, **74**, **79**, **80**, **83**

F

Field of View, **8**, **49**, **55**, **66**, **79**, **80**
File Transfer Setup, **33**
Files, **32**, **33**, **43**
Filtering, **33**, **34**
Floaty Case, **99**
Frame Rate, **37**, **70**, **79**, **80**
Frame Rates, **43**, **44**, **58**

G

GoPro, **viii**, **1**, **2**, **3**, **4**, **5**, **6**, **7**, **10**, **11**, **12**, **18**, **20**, **22**, **25**, **27**, **29**, **30**, **31**, **32**, **33**, **34**, **35**, **36**, **37**, **39**, **40**, **41**, **44**, **45**, **46**, **47**, **49**, **50**, **52**, **53**, **54**, **55**, **57**, **58**, **59**, **60**, **63**, **64**, **66**, **67**, **68**, **69**, **70**, **71**, **72**, **73**, **74**, **75**, **76**, **77**, **78**, **79**, **81**, **82**, **83**, **84**, **85**, **87**, **88**, **89**, **90**, **91**, **92**, **93**, **94**, **95**, **96**, **97**, **98**, **99**, **100**, **101**, **102**, **103**, **104**, **105**
GoPro Hero 13, **viii**, **1**, **2**, **3**, **4**, **5**, **6**, **7**, **10**, **11**, **12**, **18**, **32**, **33**, **35**, **36**, **37**, **39**, **40**, **41**, **44**, **45**, **46**, **49**, **52**, **54**, **55**, **57**, **66**, **67**, **68**, **69**, **70**, **71**, **72**, **73**, **74**, **75**, **76**, **77**, **78**, **79**, **81**, **82**, **83**, **84**, **85**, **87**, **88**, **89**, **90**, **91**, **92**, **93**, **94**, **96**, **98**, **100**, **101**, **102**, **105**
GPS, **2**, **8**, **47**, **77**, **78**

H

Handlebar, **95**, **98**
HDR, 44, **45**, 66, 69, 70, 71, 72, 74, 85
Helmet, **95**, **99**, **102**
Hiking, **98**, **99**
Horizon Lock, **38**, **53**, **55**, **57**, **58**, **60**, **86**
Hydrophobic, **15**
HyperSmooth, 4, 8, **38**, **46**, **49**, **53**, **55**, **57**, **58**, **68**, **69**, **76**, **77**, **79**, **80**, **86**, **87**, **91**, **95**
HyperSmooth 6.0, **4**, **8**, **57**, **58**, **86**, **87**

I

Image Dimensions, **38**
ISO, **44**, **45**, **46**, **72**, **76**, **83**, **84**, **95**

L

Landscape Lock, **61**, **62**
Language, **24**
LENS, **49**
Lens Cover, **11**, **15**, **96**
Lens Mod, 1, **15**, **46**, **49**, **50**, **52**, **53**, **54**, **55**, **56**, **68**, **69**, **85**, **87**, **88**, **89**, **90**, **91**
Lens Mode, **12**, **46**
Lens Mods, **5**, **9**, **52**, **91**, **102**, **103**
Lens Protection, **94**
Lenses, **49**, **85**, **90**
Light Mod, **73**, **96**, **97**, **98**
Live Burst, **66**
Live Stream, **30**, **36**
Live Streaming, **75**, **76**, **77**
Low Light, **72**, **80**
Low-light, **44**
Low-Light, **8**, **42**, **44**, **45**, **57**, **72**, **74**, **91**, **95**

M

Macro lens, **50**
Macro Lens, **46**, **50**, **53**, **54**, **55**, **68**, **69**, **85**, **89**
Macro Shots, **89**
Magnetic Latch, **11**, **51**, **86**, **93**, **101**
Media Mod, **5**, **92**, **96**, **97**, **98**
Media View, **30**
Memory Card, **19**, **21**, **74**
Microphone, **4**, **14**, **82**, **92**, **96**
Microphones, **14**, **90**, **91**
Mode, **15**, **20**, **21**, **22**, **25**, **31**, **38**, **44**, **47**, **64**, **66**, **67**, **68**, **71**, **72**, **73**, **74**, **81**, **86**

Mods, **49**, **52**, **54**, **96**, **98**, **105**
MODS, **49**
Mounting, **8**, **11**, **17**, **51**, **68**, **86**, **91**, **92**, **93**, **94**, **95**, **98**, **100**, **101**, **102**

N

ND filter, **1**, **6**
ND Filter 4-Pack, **51**, **56**
ND filters, **5**, **9**, **12**, **56**
Night Modes, **72**

O

On-Screen, **21**
Orientation Lock, **61**, **62**, **63**

P

Performance Data Tracking, **77**
Performance Sticker, **78**
Performance Stickers, **78**
Photo, **19**, **20**, **25**, **64**, **65**, **66**, **71**, **72**
Ports, **12**, **96**
Post Processing, **71**
Post-Processing, **47**, **70**, **73**, **74**
Post-Production Tips, **88**
Power, **12**, **15**, **21**, **22**, **31**, **47**, **76**, **98**, **100**, **101**
Practical Applications, **82**, **88**
Preferences, **13**, **21**, **22**, **23**, **26**, **31**, **48**, **62**, **78**
Preset Backup and Sharing, **81**
Preset Settings, **31**
ProTune, **83**, **84**

Q

Quick-Release Mounts, **95**
Quik, **29**, **30**, **31**, **32**, **33**, **34**, **35**, **36**, **75**, **76**, **78**, **79**
QuikCapture, **47**, **48**, **68**

R

Raw, **66**, **74**
RAW, **66**, **73**, **74**, **75**
RAW Capture, **73**
Rear Touch, **16**, **18**, **20**, **21**
Rear Touchscreen, **20**
Recording, **23**, **25**, **39**, **40**, **41**, **46**, **98**
Resolution, **9**, **37**, **39**, **40**, **41**, **46**, **58**, **66**, **70**, **79**, **80**, **85**

RTMP, **75**, **76**

S

SELF-TIMER, **64**
Settings, **15**, **20**, **37**, **44**, **45**, **46**, **53**, **69**, **70**, **72**, **73**, **74**, **76**, **77**, **78**, **79**, **80**, **83**, **91**, **92**
Settings Icon, **20**
Shortcuts, **21**
Shutter, **12**, **30**, **31**, **45**, **65**, **68**, **72**, **83**
Ski Pole Mount, **99**
Slo-Mo, **1**, **67**, **86**
Slow Motion, **8**, **39**, **40**, **43**, **85**
Slow-Motion, **43**, **47**, **88**, **90**
Snap and Go Magnetic Latch, **51**, **86**, **91**, **101**, **102**
Snowboarding and skiing, **99**
Social Media, **36**, **42**
Sound Profile, **81**
Speaker, **16**
Stabilization, **3**, **45**, **46**, **47**, **57**, **58**, **59**, **68**, **79**, **80**, **86**, **95**
Still Photography, **66**
Suction Cup and Clamp Mounts, **103**
Surfboard Mount, **95**, **99**
Surfing, **41**, **98**, **99**

T

TimeWarp, **8**, **86**, **91**

Touch Screen, **16**, **18**, **20**, **21**, **22**, **23**, **26**
Trimming, **33**, **34**

U

Ultra Wide, **49**, **52**, **102**
Ultra-Wide, **52**, **54**, **55**, **85**, **91**
USB, **11**, **12**, **17**, **92**, **97**, **98**

V

Video, **1**, **3**, **9**, **20**, **25**, **26**, **38**, **46**, **58**, **64**
Viewfinder, **21**
Visual Contrast, **90**
Voice Clarity, **81**
Voice Control, **22**, **23**, **24**, **25**, **26**, **31**, **68**

W

waterproofing, **10**, **55**, **77**
White Balance, **45**, **74**, **79**, **80**, **83**, **95**
Wi-Fi, **26**, **27**, **28**, **30**, **31**, **32**, **33**, **35**, **36**, **70**, **76**
WIFI, **26**
Wind Reduction, **92**
Wireless Connections, **26**, **27**
Wrist Strap, **100**

www.ingramcontent.com/pod-product-compliance
Lightning Source LLC
Chambersburg PA
CBHW082250220526
45469CB00009B/2943